IN ORDER to love

DAVID CADMAN

IN ORDER to love

A POSITION PAPER

Cosmos, Mother and Child

A Reflection upon Love for the
Guerrand-Hèrmes Foundation for Peace

*For Jill
David*

DAVID CADMAN

ISBN: 9798869676252

HOSTED BY:

The Guerrand-Hermès Foundation for Peace.

Funding for this book has kindly been provided
by the Pure Land Foundation.

As a sequel to *Love and the Divine Feminine* published by
Panacea Books, and *The Recovery of Love*
published by Zig Publishing.

Wherever possible, Zig Publishing publishes through
Creative Commons copyright. In this case, however,
since there are extensive quotations from other peoples'
work within the text, we are publishing in the traditional
manner, with copyright remaining with
Zig Publishing and David Cadman.

Contents

9	Acknowledgements
13	Preface
31	The Birth and Life of Our Universe
79	Mother and Child
91	Reflections: What does Great Love Require?
103	Appendix 1
109	Appendix 2
139	Appendix 3
153	Appendix 4

Acknowledgements

I am grateful to Bob Boisture and the Fetzer Institute in America who have provided grants for the research for this Paper, and to the Pure Land Foundation who have supported me throughout the work. I am also grateful to the Guerrand-Hermès Foundation for Peace for hosting this project as part of A Narrative of Love, and to my colleague Scherto Gill for her consistent presence and for our continued exploration of Love. My thanks go to my colleagues Dr. Vikki Lee, and Antonia Gergen for all their help in preparing the scientific (neurological, biological and psychological) description of the relationship between mother and child in utero and when the child is newborn. Thanks also to our beta reader Graham Music for his thoughtful and helpful edits and suggestions on Antonia's text. Finally, thanks to Lucy Hart for the design and layout of this text.

Dedication

This work is dedicated to my wife,
Bridget, and all that she has
helped me to know.

Preface

I have prepared *In Order to Love* to lay down some thoughts about our ways of being. I am elderly, yet find myself unwilling to yield to convention and 'leave things as they are'. I want to invite discussion and conversation about the possibility that if, between us, we have got things wrong, we might, if we try, be able to explore other ways of being. And I know that for new ways of being to emerge, we have, first, to imagine what they might be.

I am not someone who has visions or 'receives' messages, but one day in September nearly ten years ago, as I sat in my study here in Suffolk, staring at the screen of my computer, quite literally lost for words, Love spoke to me, spoke to me for some time, and I wrote down what was said. Here it is, and I offer it to you now in full because I have come to realise that it has, ever since, shaped all that I have been trying to say about Love. I would like you to read it, read it slowly, before we move on to Chapters 1 and 2 of this text:

Love said:

"I am the messenger of stars, and of river, wind and earth. Hear me. Invite me in, and for a while suppose that what I say is true. For I speak of 'Being in Love', and once upon a time is always here.

"True being arises, can only arise, from Being in Love – Great Love, divine, universal, eternal, without time and dimension, within all that is. For I am the motion, the flux, the pulse of all that is.

"Being in love, you are united with being in Love. Without this you are separated and cannot see nor speak of anything that is true. To find Truth, find me – be in love, Be in Love. To rest and be at peace, dwell in me – be in love, Be in Love.

"Mysterious, difficult to discern, there is a law, eternal, shaping all that is. It is the law to which all must be aligned. It is the realm of Goodness, which some call God. When being is true, it is aligned to Goodness – such beauty. The laws you make and live by must follow this law of Goodness. Otherwise, they will be false, unjust and harmful."

Love said:

"I am the ever-moving principle. I am given and received. The lover and the beloved dwell in Love; together, in me, they move and are one. And although I remain a mystery, sometimes you may glimpse me when, in love, and turning towards, you feel my presence, lover and beloved intertwined. At your best your love comes close to me, Divine Love, Great Love."

Love said:

"My voice unites the True and the Good, drawing all to the One, Mother and Father of all. What I tell you is the keeping of the laws of Wisdom. It is the love you have for one another; not just that you love one another, but that you love one another in accordance with the eternal law of Goodness. You have heard this before. For this is the complete and ever abiding love that runs through all that is, and which can be discerned in all that is. You cannot proceed aright unless you follow this."

Love said:

"How then might I be known? I will tell you. I can only be known in terms of my being. Which is to say: being can only be truly known in terms of my presence. To enquire of Love is to enquire into the very nature of Being.

"When the Buddha awoke from his meditation beneath the Bodhi Tree, having seen things as they really are, I was there. And when he was asked what he had seen, he replied: 'Coming to be, coming to be, ceasing to be, ceasing to be'.

"I remember hearing this. For I am the constant rising and falling of Being, a perpetual movement of separation and reunion. Being and Love are a constant rhythm of union, separation and reunion – the essential qualities of Being, held in balance and harmony by Love.

"But in your own lives, that rhythm has been lost and broken. Separation rules. Without me, without Love, without Union between the Mother and the Father, the goodness of the whole has been abandoned, leading to great harm – imbalance, disharmony, fearfulness and injustice. All of these now shape your way of being.

"And yet there is in all being a deep inclination towards reunion, the desire for which is felt in all forms of true love; for I am the impulse by which the separated may be reunited. And with this ancient purpose, all that is seeks perfection of Goodness – transcendence, moving towards."

Love said:

"Great Love is an old and lost language. And in your time, being little understood, it is difficult to speak of. Yet without Great Love nothing can be truly understood or said.

"In your disconnected world, you need to know this. Separated and apart, you find no place for me. Seeking only to have and then to have more, you find no place for me. But without me, everything disintegrates and cannot be reunited with the One.

"Whilst you may sometimes see me and feel me in yourselves and in others, it is usually no more than a glimpse, a touch. For Great Love is something other, something beyond and within all that is. Frail as you are, you cannot look upon me directly. And yet, without me nothing can truly be.

"Despite the difficulty, you must do your best to discern my motion. To do otherwise would be to live falsely and proceed in ignorance."

Hearing this, Nature came forward and said:

"I dwell in Love. For my well-being requires balance and harmony – giving and receiving, interdependence, co-operation and adaptability. My growth and decline follow a rhythmic pattern of being in which, moved by Love, there is an arising and a falling away, a continual pattern of re-formation and renewal.

"I, too, heard it: 'Coming to be, coming to be, ceasing to be, ceasing to be'. Union, separation and reunion.

"In early September, most of the flowering has ended. Summer is giving way to Autumn. Then Winter will come, and in the darkness the magic will begin, as all that is once more returns in Spring to flower again.

"Growth declines and gives back to me all I need to nourish and renew. Much wiser than you, trees and shrubs and plants all know their well-being depends upon my well-being, whole, integrated and complete. Some will flourish and others will not, each playing their part, sustaining the intricate wholeness of Being."

Departing, Love said:

"Can you learn this? Can you hear me, the voice of stars, of river, wind and earth?"

Of all that Love said on that day, the words that struck me most were: "Hear me. Invite me in, and for a while suppose that what I say is true," because to hear or accept Love as being true and of the essence, changes everything. For if we had been *governed* by Love, really governed by Love, we would not be as we are, we would not have come to where we are, with all the difficulties that we now face – climate breakdown, wildfire, flood and drought, a culture of violence and separation, and evidence of growing dis-ease, not least amongst our young people.

And so, again and again I have returned to those words that Love spoke to me: "Suppose what I say is true." And it is this supposition that is the backbone of all that I shall say in this Paper. I am not claiming a Truth with a capital 'T', something to be defended, I am sharing an exploration of a possibility and looking to see what might happen if it were to come to fulfilment, if Love came to govern all that is; and, most especially to discover what it is that Love requires of us in order that this may be so.

One result of the wisdom that came to me on that September day, was that my colleague Scherto Gill, of the Guerrand-Hermès Foundation for Peace, and I began to put together a research programme that we have called A Narrative of Love.[1] We wanted to explore the nature of Love and to find ways to practise Love more fully. The work is ongoing but, so far, it has been expressed in four publications and in the work undertaken by Scherto in the Global Humanity Foundation for Peace Institute (GHfPI) at the University of Wales Trinity Saint David (UoWTSD).[2]

The first publication was a collection of essays compiled and edited by the two of us and titled *Why Love Matters*.[3] Then came two of my own books, *Love and the Divine Feminine*,[4] and *The Recovery of Love*.[5] And then, most recently, there is Scherto's book, *Lest We Lose Love*, which is subtitled *Rediscovering the Core of Western Culture*.[6]

Published in 2016, *Why Love Matters* was a gathering of thoughts from people practising in the fields of politics, economy, health and peace, and it suggested that Love mattered because a new story was now needed to guide us, a story in which core human values such as love, respect, compassion, justice and dignity would be a necessary part of the governance of both our private and public lives. In the Foreword to this book, the late Desmond Tutu spoke of 'Ubuntu', a word used in South Africa to suggest that "humans cannot exist in isolation because we are bound together in oneness."[7] Ubuntu he said:

> …is the ultimate philosophy of good governance. Without

Ubuntu, without love and compassion, there will be no human dignity – dignity as the result of our caring for one another which underlies other moral pillars of our societies: respect, forgiveness, understanding and justice.[8]

It was said that these values would now need to be integral to our being; indeed that they could only arise from a recognition of, and an acceptance of, our essence of Love, our true being. And in the Introduction to this book, Scherto and I said this:

> We take 'Love' with a capital 'L' to be a fundamental shaping principle. It is the thread, the pulse, the ordering principle that gives shape to and is experienced by all that is.[9]

Love and the Divine Feminine, published in 2020, was an exploration of the loss of the teachings of love and the feminine as being at the heart of Western culture for some five thousand years, and in particular during the last two thousand years, when a particular kind of patriarchy and a doctrine of sin and redemption came to dominate our perception of who we are, and how we should be, dismissing the feminine, and thereby leaving a trail of suffering and destruction. For because qualities of love, compassion and a caring for others were regarded as 'womanly', as women were dismissed and disempowered, so too was Love. Much damage was done.

Acknowledging the loss of love and the feminine, in 2022 *The Recovery of Love* explored how it is that we have come to be where we are, with all the social, environmental and, indeed, economic difficulties that we face, and what it is that is required of us in order to take another direction, with the proposition that this new direction would need to be based upon Love and Right Relationship.

Then, this year, 2023, Scherto's book, *Lest We Lose Love*, has been published with its aim of enabling people to find hope in our collective capacity to value what truly matters to our common life, sustain congenial relationships amongst all, and extend our caring to other people, and other beings on the planet. Aligned to the aims of this publication, the work of the GHfPI is broadly educational and is dedicated to the promotion of collective healing, social justice and global well-being. Speaking at the launch of the Institute in 2021, Scherto focused on challenging the dominant conception of peace as an absence of violence, advancing a positive understanding of peace as being well, living well and becoming well. Her lecture also explored how global humanity must embrace an ethic of Love to engage in diversity as a pathway to collective flourishing in harmony with the thriving of other beings on the planet. The Institute is now working with UNESCO to foster this work through programmes of collective healing, and exploring global governance founded on principles of Harmony, Love and an ethics of caring.

In undertaking all of this work, Scherto and I have now come to see that something is missing. We have looked at what Love means to us, how we might be governed by it, and we have looked at how it might be expressed in practice and how it might enrich our lives, but we have not turned this matter on its head and asked what needs to be in place for Love to arise. Or rather, since the work so far suggests that Love is always present, what it is that Love requires of us, and indeed of all that is, in order that Love may be made manifest What is it that is needed if Love is to flourish, to be nurtured and expressed?

Trying to answer this question is the subject of this text, *In Order to Love*. And I have undertaken this task mindful of that voice that came to me years ago when Love said:

> Hear me. Invite me in, and for a while suppose that what I say is true.

Suppose, then, that what Love says is true.

When we speak of Love, it is always characterised in terms of relationships – 'love of', 'love for', 'in love with'. Love as a verb rather than a noun. Love always supposes 'the other' and in this it is an impulse, an energy, a force that carries information, forming and shaping relationships, and determining the quality of engagement. But many suppose that there is something beyond this, something that might be called God, or The One.[10] In this, and after many years of being troubled by it, I follow the first Epistle of John, which proclaims that "God is Love."[11] It is not that God is, amongst other things, Love, but that God *is* Love. And it is for this reason, and because the word 'God' carries such a weight of assumptions that I cannot accept, that I speak not of God but of Love as being the Ultimate Presence, the consciousness of Nature, the Universe and the Cosmos. In this way, we might say that Love is that which fosters right relationship. Some say that Love has many meanings, and that is so, but I hope that in the course of this enquiry the meaning of the Love of which I speak will become clear.

But where to begin?

There would be many possible places from which to start, not least in the teachings of the great spiritual and philosophical traditions that my colleague Scherto Gill and I have already explored in *A Narrative of Love*, including the second chapter of *The Recovery of Love* and the entire text of Scherto's book, *Lest We Lose Love*. But for the purpose of answering the question of what it is that Love requires of us, I start, in Chapter 1 of this Paper, by exploring what some cosmologists have said about the birth and life of our Universe and of our planet Earth with all its many and diverse inhabitants. Here, I begin with the writings of the Jesuit Catholic priest, geologist and archaeologist, Pierre Teilhard de Chardin. I will explain later how this came about, but I can say that, to my delight and surprise I have found that his writings on Love, with, of course, much greater authority than mine, affirm much of what I am learning about Love – for example, he affirms what I have understood of Love as being 'of the essence'. Indeed, in their commentary on Teilhard's work,[12] Louis M. Savary and Patricia H. Berne say that Teilhard described Love as a supreme energetic force that is manifested as an evolutionary law in "four stages of evolutionary love,"[13] the laws of "Attraction-Connection-Complexity-Consciousness."[14] The first two of these stages are particularly important for my work, because they see Love as energy, "a steady, powerful energy source"[15] driving and transforming not just our lives but also the life and evolution of our Universe. To my delight I find that Teilhard sees humanity's spiritual task not as being about some kind of individual salvation, but rather as enabling and supporting what is referred to as the evolutionary law of Love:

> Teilhard wants to go beyond that individual-salvation emphasis… to foster the human race's continual improvement in *learning to love*, which he sees as central to God's project for us who live on Earth.[16] (my emphasis)

In this, "Love is of its nature relational,"[17] and is part of an evolutionary process:

> …the universe is being guided and driven by [an] evolutionary law of love through the process of Attraction-Connection-Complexity-Consciousness [that is] a law that *brings things together*.[18] (author's emphasis)

My reflection on Teilhard is then followed by an exploration of two other cosmologists, Brian Swimme and Jude Currivan, both of whom are influenced by Teilhard, and both of whom accept his description of an unfolding Universe of relationships. Indeed, Brian Swimme begins by replacing the notion of a static and fixed cosmos with the notion of an ever-moving and evolving *cosmogenesis*, which, he says can be summarized as follows:

> The universe began fourteen billion years ago with the emergence of elementary particles in the form of primordial plasma, which quickly morphed into atoms of hydrogen, helium, and lithium; 100 million years later, galaxies began to appear, and in one of these, the Milky Way, minerals arranged themselves into living cells that constructed advanced life, including evergreen trees, coral reefs, and the vertebrate nervous systems that humans used to discover this entire sequence of universe development.[19]

From here, as we shall see, Swimme takes us into his own exploration of the birth and life of our Universe and in particular his collaboration with the Catholic priest and cultural historian,

Thomas Berry.

The cosmologist Jude Currivan, who studied physics and then, like Teilhard, archaeology, describes the Universe as a 'cosmic hologram' whose fundamental characteristic is 'information', or 'in-formation' as she sometimes puts it:

> The reality of our Universe, its meaningfully in-formed and holographically manifest appearance of space-time and energy-matter, emerges from nonphysical realms of causation and intelligence. From the wisdom teachings of the Upanishads of ancient India to the pioneers of quantum physics and now to the latest available science, ... our Universe is being revealed to be a great and finite thought in the eternal mind of the Cosmos.[20]

Our Universe, then, is said to be a Great Thought (my capitals) and, as my story unfolds, we will find, with some support, that I propose, or rather suppose, that our Universe is as it is because it began with an *outbreath of Love* (see Appendix 1), and that its purpose is to move from Love, through Love to Great love.

And then, because it is said to be integral to an evolving Universe, I have briefly explored the nature of 'consciousness'. In this I have primarily turned for help to the English scholar and writer, Rupert Spira, who in his book *The Nature of Consciousness*,[21] says:

> Our world culture is founded upon the assumption that reality consists of two essential ingredients: mind and matter. In this duality, matter is considered the primary element, giving rise to the prevailing materialistic paradigm in which it is believed that mind, or consciousness – the knowing element of the mind – is derived from matter.
>
> How consciousness is supposedly derived from matter – a question known as 'the hard problem of consciousness' – remains a mystery, and is indeed one of the most vexing questions in science and philosophy today.[22]

But then he goes on to say:

Ironically, in all other fields of scientific research such lack of evidence would undermine the premise upon which the theory stands, but in a leap of faith that betrays the irrational nature of materialism itself, the conviction at its heart is not undermined by the lack of supporting evidence, nor indeed by compelling evidence to the contrary.[23]

Mind, or Consciousness, precedes matter. I must remember that, because, as we shall see, Consciousness is said to be an expression of pure Love.

Having set this as a universal 'background', in Chapter 2, I then turn to something more personal. Here, I turn to another birthing by exploring what can be said about that most primal relationship, the relationship between a child and her mother, which begins within the womb and continues in the earliest months of infancy. I do this because it is my intuition that this will prove to be essential to understanding what Love is, how Love arises and is nurtured, and what it is that Love requires.

In the preparation of this part of my text, I have been blessed to be guided by Dr. Victoria Lee, a leading academic and practitioner at the Tavistock Institute in London with a specialisation in the conditions experienced by children in their early and then later lives. She is a practising and published child psychologist – a child and educational psychologist – and knows well the field and the literature. It was she who helped me to find and then supervise my research assistant, Antonia Gergen, a graduate of the University of California Santa Cruz, now living in Finland. It is Vikki who has kept an eye on our work as it has proceeded. Under Vikki's supervision, Antonia has provided a separate text (Appendix 2), which is a description of this birthing from a neurological, biological and psychological perspective. It is this text that forms the basis for my reflections in Chapter 2.

In Chapter 3, I reflect upon all that has been explored.

The position statement for this text is, therefore, as follows:

Love is the *intention* that is expressed in the evolution of our Universe; it is this intention that shapes all that is, including us; and it is this intention that is nurtured in the relationship between a mother and her child in utero and when the child is newborn. In all of this, *Love is of the essence.*

In Order to Love is the third of my texts on Love, and in undertaking it I cannot claim – not that I wish to – that 'objectivity' that academics require. I have stated my position, which is derived from my understanding that Love *is*, and in the following text my purpose is this: I want to see if there are others that support my view of Love as being of the essence, and to learn from them the ways in which Love might be further nurtured into flourishing. I admit – willingly – that even in this, I have been deliberately selective. In Chapter 1, I have been selective in the literature that I have chosen to read, and in Chapter 2 I have been content to be guided by my colleagues Vikki Lee Simpson and Antonia Gergen. Appendix 4 provides a Bibliography.

Finally, there is one more thing for me to say. Whilst all of this work was being undertaken, I met, as if by chance, a Chinese Taoist Master, Christopher Chuang, and together we began to explore what we could learn about Love from the teachings of the Tao. Most recently, a part of our work has been to establish the regular practice of a Time of Silence with Christopher and his community in China, a practice, carried on Zoom, of sitting together with his community of students, sitting in stillness and silence, and allowing a space for Love to arise. Because the Tao has played an important part in shaping my thoughts for this Paper, I would like to share some of them with you. They are set out in Appendix 3. I regard the Tao as a most important teaching for a world, a universe, that requires us to understand and become a part of 'relational being'.[24]

So, with this as a background let us begin on a grey and cold January day in 2023, mindful of those words that Scherto Gill and I wrote in the Introduction to *Why Love Matters*.

> We take 'Love' with a capital 'L' to be a fundamental shaping principle. It is the thread, the pulse, the ordering principle that gives shape to and is experienced by all that is.[25]

Endnotes

1. narrative-of-love.org.
2. This Institute is a partnership between the Guerrand-Hermès Foundation for Peace and the University of Wales Trinity Saint David.
3. *Why Love Matters: Values in Governance,* compiled and edited by Scherto Gill and David Cadman, Peter Lang, 2016.
4. David Cadman, *Love and the Divine Feminine*, Panacea Books, 2020.
5. David Cadman, *The Recovery of Love: Living in a Troubled World*, Zig Publishing, 2022.
6. Scherto Gill, *Lest We Lose Love: Rediscovering the Core of Western Culture*, Anthem Press, 2023.
7. *Why Love Matters: Values in Governance*, compiled and edited by Scherto Gill and David Cadman, Peter Lang, 2016. vii.
8. Ibid.
9. Ibid. 3.
10. A discussion of this is found in Chapter 2 of *The Recovery of Love*.
11. 1 John 4:16.
12. Louis M. Savary and Patricia H. Berne, *Teilhard de Chardin on Love*, Paulist Press, New York, 2017.
13. Ibid. 19.
14. Ibid.
15. Ibid. 22.
16. Ibid. 28.
17. Ibid.
18. Ibid. 34.
19. Brian Swimme, *Cosmogenesis: An Unveiling of the Expanding Universe*, Counterpoint, 2022, 3.
20. Jude Currivan PhD, *The Story of Gaia: The Big Breath and the Evolutionary Journey of Our Conscious Planet*, Inner Traditions, 2022, 1.

21   Rupert Spira, *The Nature of Consciousness: Essays on the Unity of Mind and Matter*, Sahaja, 2017.
22   Ibid. 1.
23   Ibid.
24   For a discussion on 'relational being' see Kenneth Gergen, *Relational Being: Beyond Self and Community*, Oxford University Press, 2009.
25   *Why Love Matters: Values in Governance*, compiled and edited by Scherto Gill and David Cadman, Peter Lang, 2016, 3.

Chapter 1

The Birth and Life of Our Universe

The Tao says:

There was something formless and perfect
before the universe was born.
It is serene. Empty.
Solitary. Unchanging.
Infinite. Eternally present.
It is the mother of the universe.
For lack of a better name,
I call it the Tao.

It flows through all things,
inside and outside, and returns
to the origin of all things.[1]

Love said:

"I am the ever-moving principle. I am given and received. The lover and the beloved dwell in Love; together, in me, they move and are one. And although I remain a mystery, sometimes you may glimpse me when, in love, and turning towards, you feel my presence, lover and beloved intertwined. At your best your love comes close to me, Divine Love, Great Love."[2]

In this chapter, I take my exploration of loving relationship to our Universe in order to see if there is, here, evidence of the presence and work of Love, and an indication of what Love might require of us. You might think that I am foolish even to attempt such an adventure, let alone speak about it. And maybe this is so. But as you will see, it was not really a matter of choice, but rather of happenchance.

The very notion – expressed not only in the great traditions of faith but also within the community of science – that there was a 'beginning' for our Universe, presumes something brought into being, and poses the question: from whence? It would seem that the answer to this question is quite literally beyond us, at least for the time being. But there is one possibility which is this: that the coming into being was brought about by an intentional force characterised by being inclined to relationships, and that one relationship led to another, on and on over a very, very long period of time, almost fourteen billion years, to bring us to where we are now. I call this force, Love, and as we shall see I have found that there is some support for this.

I have two reasons for supposing this might be so. As I have said in the Introduction, the first was given to me as a gift some years ago when Love spoke to me and I wrote down what was said. Much was spoken, but the 'verse' that struck me most was when Love said:

> I am the messenger of stars, and of river, wind and earth. Hear me. Invite me in, and for a while suppose that what I say is true.[3]

"Suppose that what I say is true." Ever since then, that has been my deepest presumption, and I now bring it to the birth and life of our Universe.

The second reason for doing so has arisen from my reading the work of three cosmologists, deliberately chosen for challenging the classic notion of a fixed 'abode'. They are: Pierre Teilhard de Chardin,[4] Brian Swimme (and his mentor Thomas Berry),[5] and Jude Currivan.[6] All three are telling a story about the Cosmos, and each proposes an unfinished and evolving Universe that in one way or another is governed by Love. We shall come to that. And both Swimme and Currivan agree on how our Universe came into being, and that, whatever else it was, it was not the Big Bang of common parlance,[7] but something more akin to an outbreath, something minute and with great particularity expressing most delicately and precisely the information required to proceed from this beginning to where we are now, and to where the Universe may go in the distant future. I have no background in science and can only be governed by that which Love spoke to me, but a 'breath' rather than an 'explosion' seems to me to be more satisfactory. It seems to me entirely possible that although at present we cannot know from whence the beginning came, it could be that it came from that unknowable inclination towards relationship to which I have already referred, and that this could be an unknowable presence of Love. Currivan suggests that the arising was akin to a Thought and that this thought, this original outbreath, has continued and now continues to be as our Universe unfolds.[8]

And perhaps, here, I should note one of the problems of speaking at all about this matter of Love, the problem of language to which I referred in Chapter 1 of *The Recovery of Love*. As soon as we begin to describe both the knowable and the unknowable, but particularly the unknowable, we are bound by the words that we have at our disposal, words that are essentially inadequate. Thus, words such as 'birthed', or even 'Love' itself, might come across as being too anthropocentric – even though they are not intended to be. So, let me say clearly that when I use these words I am hoping that you can take them as they are meant to be, as just a way of trying to express the inexpressible. Perhaps they are just the first step towards something that we may know better in times to come. I do hope so. In any event, in using these words I am aware of their limitations.

In this part of my Reflection, I should admit that my choice of texts has been mine and mine alone – although they have not really been choices for, in some extraordinary way, I did not go to them, they presented themselves to me. One thing led to another. I read commentaries on the work of Teilhard de Chardin because, although I was unaware of it being there, I found *Teilhard de Chardin on Love* waiting patiently for me on one of my bookshelves. I cannot remember how it got there, but there it was. And whilst I can no longer recall how I came to Brian Swimme and Jude Currivan, I know that I found them whilst reading Teilhard, and then attending separate webinars that they were giving. What they were saying seemed just right for me, because I knew that for Love to be 'heard' it would be necessary to challenge our dominant culture of separation, and each of them had, in one way or another, broken away from that orthodoxy to offer what are still controversial views. So there they were, and although I did not know it at the time, others would follow.

Now, having undertaken my reading of their texts, and having added one or two more, I have come to see that there are four principal questions and findings that arise:

1. What can we say about the birth of our Universe?

2. What can we say about that which gives rise to the life of our Universe, what does it tell us about the matter of relationship, and are we separate from or a part of our Universe?

3. In this exploration, what can we say about the matter of intention and consciousness?

4. What does this say about Love as being of the essence, Love being an energetic force?

What I hope to be able to show is that Love has been present from the very beginning; that our unfinished Universe is purposeful and proceeds through, and by, forms of relationship that can be described as loving, always seeking higher levels of consciousness; and that we, as humanity, have a particular role to play in this. I shall begin by sharing my reading with you, providing, in brief form, what it is that I discovered in the writings of Teilhard, Swimme and Currivan. As you will see, if you share that exploration with me, I shall try to find answers to my questions: can we say that 'Love is of the essence'; should we take Love seriously; and how might we serve Love's purpose?

And, for your further delight and interest, I encourage you to go to the texts to which I have referred. They are remarkable, and they are set out in the Bibliography.

Pierre Teilhard de Chardin

As I have said, shortly after I had published both *Love and the Divine Feminine* and *The Recovery of Love*, I found on one of my bookshelves a commentary on Teilhard de Chardin's work on Love,[9] and I began to read. As I did so, I asked myself how was it that in all my exploration of the Matter of Love I had not discovered Teilhard before? For here, sitting on my bookshelf, not hidden, but ignored, was an affirmation of all I had been trying to say. And if I had come to see that Love was 'of the essence', so, too, had Teilhard some sixty years before me. For Teilhard had then proposed that:

> ...Love is the most universal, the most tremendous and the most mysterious of the cosmic forces... Divine love is the energy that brought the universe into being and binds it together. Human love is whatever energy we use to help divine love achieve its purpose.[10]

Born in 1881, Teilhard was a Jesuit, a Roman Catholic priest, a geologist and a palaeontologist, and in his work he proposed not only that Love was the force driving evolution, but that learning to love was our true purpose.[11] This last point is important since it begins to show us what it is that Love requires of us. It's simple really, we must *learn to love*.

God, said Teilhard, had implanted a law of love in every element of nature:

> That seed of love germinates and blossoms at every stage of creation, from sub-atomic particles in a continuous evolutionary movement all the way to human beings. God's spirit continues to imbue us with attractiveness and the desire to bond with one another, to love and be loved. God's evolutionary vision of the world is that we will all one day come to love one another. In this great union of love, we will truly recognize who we were meant to be, and we will realize that love is the only way to personal and universal fulfilment.[12]

This was exactly what I wanted to hear. Well nearly so. For, of course as a Jesuit priest, Teilhard saw this evolutionary law of Love as being an expression of God. For him then, it seemed to me, there was a separation. There was God and then there was Love expressed by God. I want to say something else. As I have said, like Teilhard I, too, have been influenced by the first epistle of John in which it is said that "God is Love."[13] So, if God is supposed to be at the origin of all that is, then it can be said that Love was there, too, and that Love is the originating presence, and that the evolutionary law is an expression of Love. No separation; a unity of Love. From Love, through Love and to Love.

Not surprisingly, Teilhard's proposition of an evolving universe, which he referred to as a 'cosmogenesis',[14] brought him into deep conflict with the Catholic Church, for the classic theological description of the creation of our Universe was then that it was created once and for all by God, and that whilst those that inhabit the Earth may change, they do so within a fixed Universe, and within the overall 'design' and purpose of God. In his time, Teilhard's proposition of an evolving Universe could not be tolerated, and the conflict was such that, as a priest, he was forbidden to publish this part of his work during his lifetime. He died in 1955.

But the conflict was not just with the Catholic Church. It was also with his fellow scientists. Although they could not see his work before he died, his proposition of a universal law of Love shaping the Universe was in stark conflict with the science of his day. For, as the Franciscan Sister, Ilia Delio, says in her Foreword to *Teilhard Chardin on Love*, with the rise of modern science:

> Love fell off the radar...and took a turn for the worse in the modern age. The history of modernity and the rise of modern philosophy can be interpreted as the death of love in the cosmos.[15]

Teilhard was proposing an evolving and unfinished universe energised by Love and, as we have seen, at the core of his work was the proposition that the unfolding of the Universe followed a fourfold pattern: Attraction-Connection-Complexity-Consciousness.[16] Of these four stages, it is the first two that particularly intrigue me, for in supposing that Love arises by laws of attraction and connection (coming into union with), I begin to understand something about what it is that Love requires in order to arise and then to flourish – an open-hearted yearning for Love. Furthermore, the idea that these qualities are in some way evolutionary helps to dispel, or at least helps me to understand more about, those feelings of despair that sometimes overwhelm me when I look at who we have become and what we do. Is it, perhaps, possible that in learning more about the birth and life of our Universe we can discover how we might move on from a culture of separation to one of connection, to one of unity and collaboration, one in which Love *is*? For Teilhard was not only proposing an evolving and unfinished Universe,[17] he was proposing an unfolding Universe in which Love is the driver of its evolution.[18] Love as its impetus.

And it should be noted that Teilhard proposed that humanity has a special role to play in this unfolding. In the Foreword to the *Phenomenon*, he seeks to show the uniqueness of human life. In his words:

> Man is not simply a new species of animal...he initiates a new species of life.[19]

For humanity makes manifest both reflective thinking and a complex social life,[20] both of which contribute to higher and higher levels of consciousness, the fourth part of Teilhard's fourfold pattern of unfolding. In this then, we, humanity, are engaged in the evolution of Love.

In 1999, what was then a new translation of *Teilhard's Le Phénomènon Humain* was published. It was written by the scholar and poet, Sarah Appleton-Weber, and in the section titled 'Love Energy', she records Teilhard once more making clear that Love and a never ceasing pattern of relationships lie at the heart of the Universe. This is one of my favourite quotations from his work:

> Driven by forces of love, the fragments of the world are seeking one another so the world may come to be.[21]

And then Teilhard says:

> Love alone is capable of completing our beings in themselves as it unites them, for the good reason that love alone takes them and joins them by their very depths – this is a fact of daily experience.[22]

And:

> A love that embraces the entire universe is not only something psychologically possible; it is also the only complete and final way in which we can love.[23]

From the very beginning, then, to where we are now, Attraction has led to Connection, which in turn has led to Complexity, and then a shift in Consciousness has arisen as, again and again, higher and higher levels of consciousness have evolved. In this, plurality has sequentially given rise to unity and then energy as, one after the other, new unities have given rise to new abilities to interact:

> Countless individual subatomic particles (*plurality*) joined to form a variety of atoms (*unity*); countless individual atoms (*plurality*) joined to form a variety of molecules (*unity*); countless individual molecules (*plurality*) joined to form a variety of compounds and meta-molecules (*unity*). In each of these new unities emerged new abilities to act and interact (*energy*).[24]

Molecules have given rise to cells, cells to organisms, and organisms have evolved to become us, the last species, or perhaps one of the last, presently to have emerged so far in a long evolutionary line. In this evolution, there has been both death and life, as only those that 'fitted into' both the original impulse towards right relationships and the circumstances of the time have survived. The spur for this was, has been, and is Love, with the ongoing purpose of giving rise to ever higher levels of consciousness, whenever and wherever this may arise. And this continuing purpose has been, and is, partly our task – to enable the Universe to develop towards its ever-seeking end of Union – Love arising to Love from, and through Love to an every growing consciousness of Great love.

For Teilhard, consciousness was "awareness accompanied by an appropriate response."[25] And he regarded conscious 'seeing' to be of the utmost importance.

> To see or to perish is the very condition laid upon everything that makes up the universe.[26]

Consciousness, reflection, understanding, and becoming at-one-with, these are our key responsibilities in the unfolding of the Universe. This must be our unending enquiry and purpose, and for this we must learn to love.

What, then, have I discovered from Teilhard: that Love is of the essence, certainly; that Love has been a part of the evolution of our Universe, this was new; that the way of Love can be described as an evolutionary law of Attraction-Connection-Complexity-

Consciousness, yes; that humanity (and perhaps other beings) is co-creating this evolution, apparently so. These findings have changed what I thought was possible, and they take my work on Love from a personal or social dimension to the dimension of our Universe. I now see that we need to undertake the task of Love, not for ourselves, not even for our communities or planet Earth, but for the intended evolution of our unfinished Universe, an evolution of Love, through Love to Love.

Brian Swimme

Since Teilhard's death, and indeed quite recently, others, in part influenced by him, have also described our Universe as unfinished, unfolding and with an intention aligned with Love. One of these is the American cosmologist, Brian Swimme. In January 2023, I purchased a copy of his then recently published book *Cosmogenesis*,[27] and shortly afterwards, again as if by happenchance, I was invited to attend a webinar in which he spoke about this book – attraction to connection!

At the beginning of *Cosmogenesis*, and using as his title the same word that Teilhard had used before him, Brian Swimme says this:

> In my life as a cosmologist, my mission has been to celebrate the great events of cosmogenesis by employing the central theories of contemporary science: quantum mechanics, the second law of thermodynamics, the general theory of relativity, plate tectonics, natural selection, encephalization. These theories have enabled us to discover our cosmic genesis, which can be summarized in a single complex sentence: the universe began fourteen billion years ago with the emergence of elementary particles in the form of primordial plasma, which quickly morphed into atoms of hydrogen, helium and lithium; a hundred million years later, galaxies began to appear, and in one of these, the Milky Way, minerals arranged themselves into living cells that constructed advanced life, including evergreen trees, coral reefs, and the vertebrate nervous systems that humans used to discover this entire sequence of universe developments.[28]

As I have neither the maths nor the physics for this understanding – and had to look up more than one of the words he was using, including 'encephalization', which apparently is about an evolutionary increase in the complexity or relative size of the brain – I hoped he would not be too harsh on me. He wasn't. I had noted that he, too, was using another of Teilhard's words, the word 'complexity', a word that had been part of Teilhard's fourfold evolutionary law, and so I thought I must be going in the right direction. But I was pulled back into questions when he said that he had come to see that in studying the Universe 'out there' he had realized that he, too, was part of that evolution. He said that "he was as much a development [of the universe] as were the stars and the galaxies."[29] What might that mean?

And so I began what was in part a reading of an exploration of the universe and in part the reading of Brian Swimme's autobiography. His story begins at the University of Puget Sound in the state of Washington, on his first day as a professor of mathematics, and his exploration of the holy grail of mathematical science: "the equation synthesizing the general theory of relativity in quantum physics."[30]

At first, he sounded very enthusiastic, but the first part of his book records his gradual disillusionment with what it was that he was being asked to do, especially when a senior colleague told him that it was all worthwhile because he would be able to retire on a satisfactory pension at the age of fifty-five. Was that it? And so, as in his excitement he is beginning to understand the latest findings of science about the birth of the universe, so his frustration with the constraints within which he is being asked to work increases. Eventually, he comes to see that he must leave the University in order to be able to follow his cosmological quest.

But before he goes, whilst attending a conference on mathematical cosmology, he meets the world famous scientist, Freeman Dyson, the man who had worked with Albert Einstein at Princeton's Institute of Advanced Study, and who had made a statement that had intrigued Swimme. He had said:

> In some sense, the universe must have known, from the beginning, that we were coming.[31]

After he had spoken at this conference, Dyson was surrounded by people who wanted to ask him questions. Swimme waited and then took his chance. Hesitantly, he asked Dyson whether or not he liked the phrase 'the anthropic principle' as a way of referring to such things as the fine-tuning of the universe. Dyson's response at first seemed flat, as if he was tired. But then he said:

> Phrases like 'fine-tuning' or 'the anthropic principle' keep us in the world of classical physics. Such phrases are inadequate. The universe has evolved exquisitely enough to understand how it all happened. *That's* what needs explanation.[32]

The notion of the universe understanding how it had all happened! This was exactly what Swimme wanted to talk about. But then, as he tried to continue the conversation, he felt Dyson's interest fading, and so he stood up to make way for others and left the crowded room.

As I read this first part of the book, I shared Swimme's growing frustration that what he was increasingly wanting to explore was not being 'heard', especially by his colleagues and the trustees of the University. He began to see that if he was going to continue his work he would have to leave the security and constraints of Puget Sound and undertake an adventure of his own, an adventure captured in the following thoughts that came to him after an unsatisfactory meeting with one of his former students:

> The origin of the universe is an infinity that expands into the known universe. We don't know the meaning of a universe coming from infinity. It's the same with our knowledge of the end, with the universe expanding into an infinite future. That's what draws us on. Why couldn't I just say that to her? When I speak of the earliest moments of the universe, I am only too happy to say the expansion rate is evidence that the universe knows how to construct stars and galaxies. Well, if the universe in the form of primordial plasma knew where it was headed, why shouldn't the contemporary universe know where it is headed.[33]

Perhaps Dyson had been right, perhaps the universe did know

we were coming.

So it is that in the second part of his book Brian Swimme shares his adventure with us. At the outset, to give an indication as to where his thoughts are going, he questions whether there are 'other ways of knowing'.

> This something more, also known as "other ways of knowing" – the nonconceptual, conative, heart-centred, mystical – refers to knowledge that comes not from an objective analysis of the thing but from a communion experience with the thing, the prime illustration being the knowledge one gains from falling in love. I was wondering if these more 'subjective' ways of knowing had any place alongside mathematical science. Was it meaningful to speak of a heart-centred knowing of the origin of the universe? Would it be as real as the equations that described the universe's birth and development? Could intuitive knowledge be synthesized with mathematical knowledge to form an even deeper understanding? And if so, could I myself attain such a synthesis?[34]

It was then that he came across a book by the Catholic theologian Matthew Fox speaking about the fourteenth-century German theologian Meister Eckhart in which Fox had said that he saw "a glimpse of the universe rather than an explication of theological doctrine."[35] For Swimme, this was inspiring.

And so began an important and impulsive collaboration in which Swimme, giving up on what would have been prestigious work with MIT in Massachusetts and at Moscow State University, takes his family to Chicago so that he can give lectures at Matthew Fox's Mundelein College. He and Fox immediately set to work on a book to try and bring together the latest scientific discoveries about the universe with a theology that would take this into account.

> The assertion that science needed to reinvent itself in the wake of quantum and relativity theories was commonplace. Matt's declaration was both more radical and more controversial. He maintained that the religions of the Western world, especially Christianity, had been captured by the idea that a human's ultimate purpose is to be redeemed from a fallen world. This

fixation on escape had resulted in modern theology's slide into irrelevance, most notably among the highly educated and the young. His proposal was that Western Christianity needed to drop its obsession with getting redeemed out of the world and return to an earlier theology such as that of twelfth-century Hildegard of Bingen, who held that the universe was not 'fallen' but the primary manifestation of divine magnificence.[36]

These words of Swimme so fitted into some of my earlier work in *Love and the Divine Feminine* and *The Recovery of Love*, that I read on with enthusiasm.

It was working with Matthew Fox that led Swimme to what was to be the most important collaboration of his life, a relationship with the Catholic priest and cultural historian, Thomas Berry, and it is this relationship that takes up the remaining pages of *Cosmogenesis*. It begins with Swimme reading an article by Berry titled 'The New Cosmic Order'. And it leads to Swimme and Fox deciding they would like to invite Berry to come from New York to Chicago to give a series of lectures. Unsure of what the response might be, they decide that they will simply pick up the phone and call him. Much to their surprise and delight, Berry is there, and after some discussion he agrees that he will come. Attraction-Connection!

Some weeks later, Berry arrives in the bitter cold of a Chicago winter, dressed not in a protective overcoat but in what, as they grew to know him, he always seemed to be wearing, a corduroy jacket with leather patches at the elbows. No hat. At once Swimme is drawn to Berry, and somehow knows that what is happening is of great importance.[37] But then, when, with his usual enthusiasm, he describes to his guest the work that he and Fox are doing in bringing science and theology together, the response is unexpected. "No doubt the work that you are doing is of great importance," Berry replies:

> …[but] I, myself am pursuing a different path. I am not that interested in theology or mysticism. What interests me is the universe itself, especially its development through time.
>
> In my judgement, the greatest discovery of the last four hundred years is the time-developmental nature of our universe. Scientists have come to realize we live not in a cosmos but in a

cosmogenesis, a universe developing from a primordial simple state into ever more complex states.[38]

Berry goes on to describe how much affected he has been by the work of Teilhard de Chardin – music to my ears! – emphasising that Teilhard was a geologist rather than a philosopher, and that his work was well rooted in the 'concrete events of the universe'. Teilhard's hunt, he said, was for the meaning of life, and this always led him back to the developing universe. What had apparently fascinated him, said Berry, was the fact that "hydrogen became stellar systems with human consciousness."[39]

Swimme was stunned, for he realised that Berry was saying something he had never heard before, that the origin of the universe was somehow linked to human consciousness. At first he was defensive, thinking that what had been said would threaten his work with Fox. But then he relented, for, as he later realised, there was no threat, but rather there was a marvellous opportunity. Indeed this conversation, and his unfolding relationship with Berry, would change his work for ever. His mind was ablaze, as he now began to understand what Berry had meant by 'a new cosmological myth'. The conversation continued and as it was ending Berry said:

> If we force science's findings into earlier philosophical or spiritual categories, we will unknowingly throw away the best parts. To give birth to a new cosmological story requires a profound creativity. Everything in Western civilization must be put on the table for discussion and reevaluation.[40]

As Berry continued with his lectures, Swimme heard him say that the contemporary stories of both science and theology were wrongly centred, too much focused on the human agenda and dangerously unaware of the need to take account of the planetary dimension.[41]

Swimme listened and listened, and the more he heard the more he knew that this was where he wanted his work to be. Somewhat fearfully, because he knew that this would mean yet more disruption for his family, he realised that he would have to follow this man in his corduroy jacket to New York to work with him there. He was right to be worried, but in the event it was his wife, Denise, who, understanding that her husband had at last found his teacher, with great courage and love insisted that they should go.

And so Swimme and his family went to New York and to the three-story Victorian mansion in which Berry now lived. The house had been condemned and listed for demolition, but the Passionate monks, with whom Berry worked, had saved it, restored it and made it into a residence for four of their own. Swimme had assumed that Berry would know why he had come, but, as he began to speak of his work it seemed as if he didn't. Instead, Berry began to outline that which he thought was needed – a new story. He shared with Swimme his copy of Teilhard de Chardin's major work – perhaps this was Teilhard's *The Phenomenon of Man* – and as he did so, he said:

> The Great achievement of Teilhard is to recognize that science has discovered cosmogenesis ... Everything, is [evolving]; even the universe as a whole is evolving from its relatively simple beginning to more complex forms.
>
> The universe is coming to know itself. That is the meaning of the human species. The meaning of our existence is to provide a space in which the universe can reflect upon and activate itself in conscious self-awareness. This can only be achieved by a unified humanity, which Teilhard called the noosphere.[42]

Berry continued to describe his version of the evolution of the universe in terms of a complex network of relationships through which humanity would come to know itself, ending by saying that this was the spiritual task of our time, and telling Swimme that this was why he had struggled to fit in at the University of Puget Sound:

> It seems to me [he said] your role is not in science exactly but in cosmology. Your destiny is to tell the universe story.[43]

That evening, as he drove back to where he and his family were staying, Swimme knew that this is what he wanted to do and this is who he wanted to be his guide. Berry had made it clear that although he thought there would be resistance to the story, that the new story had to be told, in order to bring about the awakening of a new era:

> The exciting action of our time [he said] is the creation of a cosmological form of humanity. ... Come to understand you are not a scientist. You are not an American. You are not male. You are not even primarily a human. First and foremost you are a cosmological being.[44]

What a thought!

The task began in late 1982, and Berry, of course wearing his brown corduroy jacket, began his instruction. To start with, he introduced Swimme to the writings of Dante, because he thought it important that Swimme should study the work of someone from his own cultural background, someone who, in his time, had described a kind of cosmology.

I was struck by one sentence spoken by Berry – and I assume Swimme was, too, since he chose to record it:

> Even one act of love on the part of a single human results in a chorus of praise by the community of saints and angels in Dante's heaven.[45]

And then, this:

> Earth is more alive, more intelligent, more beautiful, more sensitive, more complex than any galaxy or star or planet we have examined. Earth then can be considered the primary revelation of what the universe is aiming to establish.[46]

Perhaps we should add to the claim of "primary revelation," the words, "as far as we know."

Swimme had to tell Berry that he was struggling to grasp what was being said. And, indeed, Berry accepted that most individuals throughout our advanced civilizations would find his description of their world and their universe difficult, if not impossible, to understand. Nevertheless, he insisted that trying to provide this understanding was the story that Swimme had to tell. How far was this from teaching mathematics as the University of Puget Sound?

The work went on, and it seems that it continued to challenge what Swimme thought he knew about the universe and our relationship with it. He and Berry continued to discuss Dante and Thomas Aquinas, the extinction of species and our limitations in trying to understand what was happening. Much of what Berry said about the dangers that he saw for the future of humanity were troubling, and much of it Swimme found difficult to share with others. But Berry told him that humanity was not separate from the universe, that the universe and the Earth had constructed us – for a purpose.

One time, when they are travelling together, Swimme asks: "[Is] this what you mean when you say we humans have to stop hogging all the noble qualities for our ourselves, things like love and generosity and spirituality?"[47] Berry reaches over and taps Swimme's forearm with his index finger. He is smiling. "Simply that," he says. Swimme then asks if that means that the Sun is generous. "Certainly," replies Berry.[48] And then he continues:

> If in each second, the Sun is deluging us with light, and if that light has powered every act of human love and generosity since the beginning of humanity, shouldn't we be free enough to call this bestowal of light generous?[49]

Once more, this was making Swimme feel giddy! The Sun is generous?

In another, later, conversation Berry had said that the elegance of the universe was what he called "a cosmic form of intention,"[50] and Swimme had replied by suggesting that they were back with the generosity of the Sun. What Berry said next is, I suggest, of such importance that it must we quoted at length, not least because it raises the matter of 'intention':

> As you say, the crucial element here is that of *intention*, for that is how we identify acts of generosity. We need to understand that the universe can intend something even before human consciousness

emerges. In the earliest moments of time, the universe was filled with chaotic interactions, violent collisions, and chance events, but even so, the universe found its way to construct complex spiral galaxies. There was no conscious mind intending a spiral galaxy, that is true. *But intention lives at the level of matter itself.* Matter is not inert or passive. *Matter's intrinsic dynamism is the cosmic form of intention.* As you can see, I'm using the 'intention' with respect to energy, the same energy physicists and cosmologists study, the energy of the big bang. I am making the simple assertion that the ferocious energy at the beginning *aimed* at constructing stars and galaxies.[51] (my emphases)

I think I have got this right when I say that what Berry was saying suggests that things are intended to happen and that they can only happen when the time is ready for them. Until then, they remain a potentiality.

In the story that Brian Swimme tells, he is certainly saying that Berry thought our Universe was readying for a new way of what Teilhard had referred to as 'seeing', one brought about by cosmogenesis.[52] Furthermore, by helping us experience ourselves as modes of the universe we would come to play our part in that unfolding. That is, says Swimme, what the new story of cosmogenesis offers.[53] The ongoing evolution seems always to begin with attraction. The act of attraction is primary.[54] Attracting, said Berry, is the universe acting, that's all that can be said.[55]

Swimme was now beginning to understand how important this matter of Attraction was, and how it resonated with the writings of Teilhard de Chardin:

> [I realized that I] was composed of attractions [he said]. If the elementary particles had not been attracted to one another to construct the light atoms, I would not exist. If the atoms had not been attracted to one another to construct the stars and galaxies, I would not exist. If the minerals of the rocky planet had not been attracted to one another to construct living cells, I would not exist. We live inside that nested sequence. At the base of our experience, we are an attraction inside an attraction inside an attraction.[56]

This matter of 'intention' and 'attraction' is compelling.

Berry suggested to Swimme that there were four eras of cosmic evolution: the birth of the universe; stars and galaxies; living Earth; and human consciousness.[57] And he suggested that traditional ways of thinking about this had to be relinquished, setting aside notions of a fixed cosmos for "a cosmogenesis, where the creativity of the universe is the fundamental meaning."[58] That is what it is all about.

One evening sitting together in the kitchen of Berry's house, talking about death, Berry, once again, returned to the writings of Teilhard de Chardin:

> For Teilhard [he said], development through time is the primary revelation. It is the fundamental source of meaning in the universe. By development he means the cosmic and organic evolution as discovered by scientists, but he includes his conviction that the process of evolution is entwined with *the process of love*, an idea he attempts to capture in his neologism, 'amorization'....[59] (my emphasis)

This might be so, and Berry thought that although humanity was unable to understand the deepest workings of the universe, one day it might.[60] Particularly with its reference to a 'process of love', I hope that this is true.

Seeing the emphasis on relationship and attraction in their work, I was wondering whether Berry and Swimme would say anything more about Love. They seemed to be coming close, but not actually saying so. Then I found it, right towards the end of the book. One of the last chapters was entitled 'Cosmological Love', but it was short, and spoke mainly about the generosity and sacrifice of the universe as the Sun gives its warmth unconditionally, and as stars die in the process disbursing their treasures of elements "in a form of cosmic love that enables the future to emerge."[61] I got the point, but was disappointed that there was not more.

In the last pages of his book, Swimme begins to summarize all that he has learnt from working with Berry. The universe, he says, rests on *relationship*:

> The first elementary particles, such as protons, neutrons, and electrons, deepened their relationships and gave birth to a trillion galaxies. No new particles came along. It was done by the original set. I need to say it again. These particles constructed the galaxies by doing one thing: *deepening their relationships*. This mysterious synergy happened again with the emergence of life. Unicellular organisms, each one smaller than the sharp end of a pin, entered into relationships with each other and ended up constructing lions. There is the great mystery. In relationship with another, your deeper identity is ignited. Only by entering into communion with someone outside yourself can you find your true self…In our universe, ultimate creativity rests upon the union of things.[62] (author's emphasis)

And he finishes by saying:

> Our minds will be challenged to make the figure-ground transformation: The inner is looking at the outer, which has given birth to the inner. That is the heart of cosmogenesis. Looking at processes that give birth to our looking. Looking at processes that gave birth both to the carbon of our eyes and the thinking of our minds. As we integrate this revelation into our lives, we ingest an ocean of energy. Though floating in space on a tiny planet, we are also the universe as a whole that has achieved self-awareness … The universe out there gave birth to this new awareness. These phrases simply state what mathematical and observational cosmologists have discovered: when we look at the night sky, we are looking out at that which is looking.[63] (author's emphases)

Disappointed as I was that nothing more had been said about Love, I need not have worried, for in some of the early pages of the book that Brian Swimme wrote in 2001, and dedicated to Thomas Berry, there it was. *The Universe Is a Green Dragon*,[64] was written as a dialogue between an old man called Thomas and a youth – the old man seemingly being Berry and the youth, I would say, being Swimme.

Early in the story, the youth asks the old man what is the fullest destiny of humanity, and the old man replies that it is:

To become love in human form.[65]

And that:
The journey out of emptiness is the creation of love.[66]

There it was. At last what I had been hoping for, an affirmation of Love as being 'of the essence' and shaping all that is.

And this section of the book ends with the youth asking Thomas what he means by love, and to my delight the next section is titled 'Allurement'. Thomas says:

Love begins as allurement…this primary attraction of each part of the universe for every other part."[67]

"The attraction is love?" asks the youth. To which Thomas replies:

"Start here: on the cosmic scale, an attraction exists.[68]

This second section of the first part of *The Green Dragon* explicitly turns to the matter of Love, and makes clear that whether we speak of love, attraction or allurement – and some will find one description more meaningful than another – there can be no doubt these qualities of Love, qualities that incline towards relationship, were there at the origin of the universe, and have been and are in the multitude of relationships from there until now. Indeed, at one point Berry makes clear that the activity of Love is "basic to the universe."[69] And whilst I say that some will find one description more meaningful than another, I do not say that which one they choose does not matter. Each description will come with its own presumptions, and that is why I choose to speak of Love as always 'being inclined towards relationships.'

So, even though they may have used words like 'attraction', 'generosity' or 'allurement' rather than Love with a capital 'L', as I do, it seems to me that Berry and Swimme are proposing that Love is a significant and necessary force in the birth and life of our Universe; that we inhabit a universe that flourishes on a *reality of relationships*. And thus, it seems, that my proposition of Love as being of the essence is well founded, as is the proposition of a necessary relational being, which I, too, suggest in the *Recovery of Love*.

Of course, one question that always arises, and arises in *The Green Dragon* is: how do we get from acceptance of Love as a principle to Love being part of our everyday action and practice? The answer to this is, I think, less difficult than we suppose. In every culture, there are presumptions about this, but many of these presumptions are the same, and seem to imply a manner of being in which the care of others in qualities such as loving-kindness, compassion, patience, humility, honesty and trust, are not only desirable but are necessary qualities. These codes of behaviour are found in the Christian beatitudes and in the Buddha's divine abiding. Indeed, the chapter on Love in *The Recovery of Love*[70] makes clear that such qualities are well known and universal in all the great spiritual traditions. However, the very fact that so many people find that they have to ask this question points to the poverty of our contemporary cultures where the rights of the individual rather than the command that we should love one another are assumed to be paramount. Following Teilhard, it is clear in Swimme's work with Berry that it is not only that each of us should be mindful of the needs of others, our local communities, and Earth herself, but that we should also be mindful of the needs of our Universe. They emphasize that we are not in any way separate. We, and all that is, *are* our Universe.

If Teilhard had given me an insight into a universal law of evolution, Swimme and Berry describe an evolving reality of relationships in which Love is always at work and in which humanity plays a part.

Jude Currivan

In her book, *The Cosmic Hologram*,[71] published in 2017, the cosmologist, Jude Currivan, introduces two new concepts: that the Universe is a cosmic hologram; and that the Universe is formed by patterns of information and harmonic order. She suggests that our Universe is:

> ...a cosmic hologram embodying its innate attributes of self-similar patterns of information and harmonic order that underlie all physical appearances on all scales of existence. ... [and that] information, consciousness, and ultimately cosmic intelligence are the ground states and all-pervasive fundaments of the world.[72]

Like Teilhard and Swimme, Currivan describes an intentional and purposeful Universe, which is patterned, ordered and *relational*. From its origin, which rather wonderfully she calls not the Big Bang but the Big Breath, or even just a Breath that was minutely small,[73] the Universe evolves over 13.8 billion years from its very beginning to the present, and the information needed to do so is contained in that first and continuing outbreath, moving from the simplest to the most complex forms. In other words, she says:

> ...our Universe is composed not from the all-pervasive presence of merely arbitrarily accumulated data and accidental processes, but ordered, patterned, relational, meaningful and intelligible in-formation, exquisitely balanced, incredibly co-creative, staggeringly powerful, and yet fundamentally simple.[74]

And this evolution, she says, has been the story of "progressive self-awareness,"[75] higher and higher levels of individuated consciousness, which, of course, contribute to the higher and higher consciousness of the Universe as a whole. As we have seen in the writings of both Teilhard and Swimme, this story has become increasingly accepted within science and elsewhere. And I would say that it describes a realm that is relational and intentional, one that is governed by Love. Teilhard called it the 'noosphere', a victory of love over fear:

> Teilhard perceived such a noosphere as embodying the victory of love over forces of fear. Indeed he considered that 'love is the affinity which links and draws together the elements of the world. ... Love, in fact, is *the agent of universal synthesis*.[76] (my emphasis)

Later in this same chapter of her book, Currivan makes another controversial but for me enlightening point about the relationship between the creator and that which is created, when she says:

> We've arrived at a point where, given the ubiquity of consciousness, it seems clear that asking who or what makes our Universe is the wrong question. For progressively, our scientifically based understanding is showing that there's no "real" separation between maker and what's made; the appearance of such division is solely the perspective from which the individuated aspects of consciousness may view their own holographic and holarchic imagery.[77]

The eternal intelligence of the cosmic mind, she says, finds a finite expression through the dynamic co-creativity of our Universe.

> Its existence, experiences, evolution, and eventual demise is as a unified and non-locally cognizant entity, one of the finite such expressions of the Oneness of all that is, has ever been, and ever will be.
> Thus each of us is a microscopic and unique expression playing our own co-creative role in the unfolding self-awareness of the consciousness of our finite Universe and ultimately of the infinite Cosmos.[78]

Such a perception, she says, used only to be found amongst the religious or spiritual, but now scientific discoveries are coming to the same conclusion. What she refers to as 'God', and I would call 'Love', is not 'out there' but rather within and beyond all that is.

In her *Story of Gaia*,[79] Currivan continues to explore the evolution of our Universe (13.8 billion years old) and, especially, the birth of Gaia (4.5 million years old), reinforcing her utter rejection of the notion that this evolution has been random.

> The big bang wasn't big and it wasn't a bang.
> Instead of our Universe beginning in the implicit chaos of a 'bang,' it was born in a miniscule and incredibly simple and ordered state.[80]

Indeed, she reminds us that even if fundamental physical attributes and relationships had been different by the smallest amount, our Universe would never have been able to exist, let alone go on to evolve.[81] It is through, and only through, *the ongoing relational patterns of attractions and connection* that life has come from its very beginning to where we are now.

You may recall that, in the Introduction to this book, I said that in exploring Love we were bound to explore the world of relationships – as there is no other world. It is, therefore, encouraging to find this being confirmed in Currivan's *The Story of Gaia* and, indeed, in the writings of Teilhard and Swimme. The overwhelming evidence of its innate intelligence, Currivan says:

> ...reveals a Universe that essentially exists to evolve from simplicity to ever-greater complexity and an evolutionary journey on universal and individual levels of sentience....
>
> The conclusion based on all the evidence...is that mind and consciousness aren't something that humans and other animals have but what we and the whole world literally are. And that the appearance of our Universe arises from cosmic mind and consciousness *expressed and embodied in meaningful relationships* at all scales of existence...[82] (my emphasis)

Then there is this in her opening to Chapter 2, titled 'Ancestors'. I rather like it:

> In the womb-like long night of the early Universe, and over hundreds of millions of years, primeval hydrogen and helium, traced with small amounts of lithium and even tinier amounts of beryllium, continued to cluster under the attractive influence of gravity. Within their gaseous contractions of lithium, small differences in mass resulted in different rates of infall. Converting part of their energy into rotation, they began to spin, becoming ever denser and hotter eddies as they coalesced into still-dark protostars, nestling within the surrounding void.[83]

The "womb-like long night," now I am starting to get it. And the spiralling clusters of gas in the surrounding void. I'm beginning to feel I might have seen this! But, of course, I haven't, unless I remember it in some part of my body made of star dust. And so it has gone, attraction and connection creating atoms and molecules, one energetic merger after another, until, in time, long long time into the future, the requisite conditions arise for Gaia to host the emergence of organic life in a process of continuous collaborative evolution – attraction and connection, again and again and again.[84]

Currivan describes these vast events in a language that is sometimes more like poetry than prose. It is almost as if she uses such a language because it has to be used to evoke the sheer magnificence of what is happening, perhaps touching something deep inside each one of us that is a memory: life emerging from and returning to a darkness we cannot describe; the ongoing evolutionary impulse and emergence of ever-greater complexity,[85] millions and millions of years passing, billions of years passing as evolution moves a step at a time, always working by collaboration, always moving from simplicity to complexity over a period of almost fourteen billion years. Its almost impossible to imagine such a long time, but we must do so if we wish to understand our own place in the story of our Universe – our part in the "long-term relationships and stable resonance,"[86] of our solar System, as Currivan describes them, all held within the gravitational influence of the Sun and the all-pervasive electro magnetic field of the Sun's heliosphere, which reaches to the outer limits of what is called the Oort cloud, a cloud of icy planetesimals (solid objects and debris disks) that surrounds the Sun.[87]

And it is these resonances, says Currivan that have been extraordinarily beneficial in maintaining stability for billions of years,[88] and for Gaia, have been essential for the emergence and evolution of her organic children.[89] Even in the most turbulent times, this story of Gaia is a drama of *relationships* and of cooperation, a purposeful working together and to one end – ever more complexity and consciousness.

The story of Gaia reveals a world of familial bonds, far from the supposed conflict and separation proposed as a universal truth by our dominant patriarchy of separation. For, as Currivan puts it:

> The elemental profusion that Gaia embodies pervade the rocks and minerals of her geosphere, the waters of her hydrosphere, the

snow and ice of her cryosphere, and the air of her atmosphere. Each plays their dynamically interdependent and coordinated roles to support, and be reciprocally supported by, the emergence of the organisms of her biosphere; together they form the entirety of her sentient and evolving gaiasphere.[90]

Currivan speaks of deep levels "of intelligent causation and intention,"[91] which give meaning to our Universe, which I take to arise from the originating Breath, and which are evolving into ever-higher and higher levels of consciousness. This evolution proceeds from an early and long-lived pre-atomic state, moving from atoms to molecules and then to compounds and cells, which in turn become organic life, from the simplest formations to the more complex and then still more complex, which includes all the children of the biosphere, including us.

> The traits of all organic cellular life…involve their abilities to assemble, structure, repair, and replicate themselves to differentiate themselves from their surroundings, and to energize their life processes through metabolism.[92]

Thus, not exclusively, but substantially, the story of Gaia proceeds not through random mutations but by processes of "vital collaboration."[93] Indeed, as Currivan suggests:

> …there cannot be an understanding of such evolutionary processes while attempting to separate a biological entity from its environment. In complete contrast to the neo-Darwinism model, entire ecosystems are increasingly being revealed to be in intimate *co-evolutionary and dynamic partnership*, not only inclusive of their biological entities but with the entirety of the gaiasphere and in even wider relationships with Sol and Luna.[94] (my emphasis)

From the beginning of organic life we have progressed not, as our dominant culture suggests, by a survival of the fittest, but, by and large, by a survival through co-operation and collaboration of the most fitting. Furthermore, it is becoming clearer and clearer that in this we share a single consciousness, and that mind and consciousness aren't something we have, but are quite literally what we and the whole world are.[95] Our story is, and has always has been about: "[How] the innate evolutionary impulse of our Universe continues to in-form the emergence and evolution of organic life-forms,"[96] in time birthing "the most complex microcosms of its inherent intelligence yet known."[97]

For me, that 'impulse' is 'Love at work'. Love, with its inclination to gather together and nurture, is the evolutionary language of the Universe. The story is one of collaboration, one of *relating* and *relationships*, which, by necessity or not, have included symbiotic processes.

> As Gaia's biosphere continued to evolve, collaboration between her organic children has been a constant and fundamental factor. In numerous situations …organisms have cooperated rather than competed with each other…[98]

Indeed, throughout Currivan's *The Story of Gaia*, there are many wonderful examples of collaboration, of mutuality and even self-sacrifice. The stories are fascinating. For example some of the earliest and simplest organisms, slime moulds, are said to "embody an innate collective and distributed intelligence."[99] But not only this, for our Universe, says Currivan, is *"innately intelligent and inherently alive"* (my emphasis),[100] and, imbued with a consciousness which moves incessantly from the simple to the complex, and from the complex to an increasing self-awareness. Indeed, one might say that higher and higher levels of consciousness (whatever that might mean – but which I take to be Great Love), is what our Universe is seeking and becoming. If this is so, then it seems to me that that the material world will increasingly be discovered to be no more than an outer garment, and that whilst this outer garment might, over very long periods of time, degrade and wither away, our shared consciousness – as it becomes a consciousness of Great Love – will remain forever as part of the Cosmos. Love will return to Love.

With the ongoing evolutionary impulse becoming embodied in the biosphere, Currivan suggests that what we are now seeing is:

…how the entirety of Gaia's inherently interconnected gaiasphere embodies dynamic and co-evolutionary collaboration. The waves of her evolutionary impulse are literally pulsed through epochs of relative quietude and times of radical transformation.

In the beginning, fourteen billion years ago, the outbreath of Love placed seeds of consciousness into time and space. These seeds remained dormant, or at least were not expressed for a long, long time. However, four or so billion years ago, Gaia was born and then began to bring forth life, in time birthing the first shoots of that consciousness. According to Currivan, over all of this time "underlying in-formational and causative attractors"[101] have been guiding the flow with "waves…of unfolding potential increasingly venturing onto a shore of expression and embodied sentience."[102] The progression has been slow, with "periods of equilibrium interspersed, or punctuated, by radical and often catastrophic change,"[103] guided, it would seem, through increasing diversity and sentience, by "an innate and informationally intelligent strategy to pulse complexity through the evolutionary process and with the entire gaiasphere in dynamic and co-evolutionary partnership to do so."[104] Currivan also refers to the *pulse* of the Universe. She calls it "an evolutionary pulse,"[105] and refers to it as "a story of cosmic mind and consciousness."[106]

Reading this, I recall the words Love spoke to me those years ago: "For I am the motion, the flux, the pulse of all that is."[107] Is this the same 'pulse' to which Currivan refers? I believe it is.

Currivan describes humanity's first appearance as a significant evolutionary shift, which aligns to Love:

> In Ardi, one of our first hominin relatives, we may be seeing a cognitive leap to a deeper level of emotional relationship and cooperative involvement, which is innate in our origins as humans. *We seem to have been built for love.*[108] (my emphasis)

She then says:

> …hominins from their earliest time have formed pair-bonds, families, and cooperative social groups.[109]

I believe this to be so, for, as Umberto Maturana also suggests in *The Biology of Love*,[110] the need for longer periods of parental care in early childhood may well have led us to a natural inclination towards familial bonding and social cohesion.

Indeed, as Currivan goes on to say:

> Gaia has progressively nurtured empathy and emotional attachments in her biosphere. In the cooperative and loving relationships of mates, parents, and offspring, of families and communities, she has embedded circles of caring. Bacteria, insects, and fish cooperate to look after others of their communities, especially the vulnerable. And in the altruism observed in rats and monkeys, the grieving of elephants not only for their own kin but for a human carer, the self-sacrifice of a human stranger, and the protection [from orcas] of others not of their own species by humpback whales…, the circles of care further expand as spirals of compassion.[111]

As we shall see, being born for Love will be the conclusion of my exploration of the relationship between a mother and her child in the next chapter of this Paper.

Finally, in asking herself the question of 'why' this is so, Currivan says of the story of the Universe:

> It tells of a Universe that learns through its holographic and holarchic manifestation, and through its explorative, experiential, and evolutionary reflections to further know itself. Its innate Unity, through the co-creative appearances and tensions of its dualities with their universal masculine and feminine attributes, then reconciles in the trinities of their child expressions. Their flourishing, in the diversity and complexity of its ongoing journey, will eventually come full spiral: from Unity to Unity in diversity, to a re-membered Unity in belonging, and an ultimate return to

Unity.[112]

From Love, through Love to Love.

And so, whilst affirming an evolving Universe of relationships, and following Teilhard's pattern of Attraction-Connection-Complexity-Consciousness, Currivan adds to the story: first, like Swimme, by speaking of a minutely small Breath[113] and not a Big Bang; secondly, by speaking of the notion of a flat, in-formed and holographic Universe, with an evolutionary impulse: and, thirdly, by speaking of humanity, as an essentially loving species, as being part of that evolution. I now know,[114] that Currivan, like Teilhard, also accepts the essential place of Love in the unfolding of our Universe.

Rupert Spira

Throughout these stories of the birth and life of our Universe, there are many references to consciousness. Indeed, higher and higher levels of consciousness are presented as the entire purpose or intent of our Universe. And so, for guidance as to what this consciousness might be, I turned to the spiritual teacher and philosopher, Rupert Spira. Again I struggled. It is not that what Spira says is difficult per se, it is that my mind is – perhaps all our minds are – inevitably, and to some considerable extent, shaped and limited by dominant and long-lived conventions that prevent a true understanding of consciousness. We are inclined to think of it as an object, something we *have*, rather than something that is without form, something we *are*. And so, even if I am challenging conventions with my writings on Love, I am limited by those conventions, and coming to understand the true nature of consciousness, the true nature of who we are, the relationship between consciousness, mind and matter, is not easy – well not for me.

Consciousness, or awareness, says Spira, is an ever-present knowing that cannot be described as an object.

> Whatever it is that knows objective experience can never itself be known or experienced objectively.[115]

He also says:

The essential discovery of all the great spiritual traditions is the identity of Consciousness and Reality, the discovery that the fundamental nature of each one of us is identical with the fundamental nature of the universe.[116]

In all of this, consciousness precedes matter; matter is derived from it, and the only reality is consciousness. In an age of materialism – and observing the consequences of materialism – we can see that understanding that this is so is of vital importance. For if we are to fully understand the question 'who are we?' or fully understand the birth and life of the Universe, we must set convention aside and a find new way of knowing and being, one that acknowledges and embraces more entirely this Reality.

As Spira put's it:

I believe that the materialist paradigm, which has served humanity in ways that do not need to be enumerated here, can no longer accommodate its evolving intelligence... Nor can its host, the earth, any longer survive its degradation...A new paradigm is required.[117]

For such a shift to arise, it behoves us to understand the nature of consciousness and its relationship with mind and matter:

...consciousness [says Spira] is the fundamental, underlying reality of the apparent duality of mind and matter, and the overlooking, forgetting or ignoring of this reality is the root cause of both the existential unhappiness that pervades and motivates most people's lives and the wider conflicts that exist between communities and nations.[118]

And in an edited transcript of a lecture he gave in 2015 he says:

...consciousness is that in which all experience appears, that with which all experience is known and that out of which all experience is made.[119]

It seems to me that this places Consciousness with a capital 'C', as I have placed Love with a capital 'L', at the very core of existence, the 'essence of being'.

In searching for what he might say directly about Love, I found that in *The Heart of Prayer*, he says:

> …love is God's nature; it is the prior condition of all relationship.[120]

For me – and, of course, I cannot speak for Spira – this seems very much like my notion of Love. Indeed, as I understand him, Spira's ungendered God, is "the fundamental nature of the universe,"[121] which, since he accepts that love is God's nature, seems to affirm my own proposition that Love is of the essence.

Spira puts it this way. He says that in consciousness knowing itself as everything, "this condition could be called Love."[122] And later he says that our awakening, which is the moment when the emptiness of consciousness recognizes itself as the fullness of our experience, is:

> …the path of Love.[123]

So, am I right in thinking that this essential and ever present Consciousness might be called Love, and where we speak of Consciousness, we might speak of Love? Perhaps, for if this is so, and if as Teilhard, Swimme, Berry and Currivan suggest, our Universe is ever seeking higher and higher levels of Consciousness, it would mean that we *can* say, and I *do* say, that our Universe is seeking higher and higher levels of Love.

However, and this is quite a large 'however', this might not be sufficient, for Spira says that such a view does not rid us of our materialism. He insists that even to say that the universe is conscious is to remain trapped in materialism. To say that the universe is conscious, he says, is 'panpsychism'. For:

> The universe is not conscious; consciousness is the universe.[124]

And later:

> Only consciousness really is. The apparent existence of the

universe is consciousness itself – indivisible, self-aware being – refracted through the activity of the mind.[125]

Even so, from what Spira has said about the relationship between Consciousness and Love, I am left wondering if I could say this: the universe is not Love, Love is the universe; and only Love really is? However, that would mean that Love would then have to be formless and indescribable. I confess that, for the present, this remains beyond me. I have only a glimpse of what it might mean.

Fortunately, Spira does say that the panpsychism of which I think I may be guilty, is a stepping stone. Well that's something I suppose! He says:

> Panpsychism is a stepping stone that will, hopefully, at least usher in a new paradigm in which our model of the universe starts with and is built upon consciousness itself. Sooner or later our culture must wake up from the dream of materialism, of which panpsychism is a subtle extension, and establish consciousness in its rightful place as the absolute reality of all that seems to be. The universe is consciousness itself: one seamless, indivisible, self-aware whole in which there are no parts, objects, entities or selves.[126]

Until that time comes, it seems to me that if, as Spira suggests, there is some kinship between Consciousness and Love, it is worth exploring what it would mean if we were to suppose that this formless and indescribable quality is – in ways that I cannot yet see – Love. After all, that is what Love said to me: "hear me, invite me in, and for a while suppose that what I say is true."[127]

Our being is Love's being.

Conclusions

Taken together, all of these findings, all that I have read of Teilhard, Swimme, Berry, Currivan and then of Spira, affirm my original proposal of Love as being 'of the essence of all that is,' and that our Universe is, indeed, made of a continuing and continuous flow of relationships, or of what I might call relatedness and connectedness

— Teilhard's Attraction-Connection-Complexity-Consciousness. I can also say that what I have now learnt reinforces many of the words of Love spoken to me in the quietness of my study. It is almost as if I have now discovered that ever since Love spoke to me I have been attuning myself to the work and thoughts of others; as if unknowingly I had heard what they were saying.

As I have said before, the words of Love that most struck me those years ago were: "invite me in and for a while suppose that what I say is true." But, now, having read what I have read, and looking back at what Love said, a number of other words spoken to me by Love catch my attention, words that spoke of Love as "divine, universal, eternal, without time," of Love as "the pulse of all that is," and of a Love that "shapes all that is." These words, and those that spoke of Love as "an ever-moving principle" and "a constant rhythm of union, separation and reunion," seem to fit with all that I have now learnt of an unfolding universe shaped by relatedness and Love. And were not the words spoken by Love about Love's "deep inclination towards reunion" very much like Teilhard's words in *Phenomenon*?

> Driven by forces of love, the fragments of the world are seeking one another so the world may come to be.[128]

I think they are.

However, now that I know what I know, I am still left with the question of what it is that Love requires. I have a sense that this will need a new kind of looking, and in this, I was struck by something that Brian Swimme said about the fact that the Universe knew we were coming,[129] and that our Universe is a "cosmic force of intention."[130] If that is so, then the Universe must know what comes next, or at least what is the natural consequence of its intention of moving towards higher levels of consciousness; so that, in a sense, we are not only propelled forward by purpose, but we are drawn forward by what is intended, drawn by Love towards not only Love, but what will become known in its fulfilment as 'Great Love'.

When we ask what Love requires, this is important. For instead of looking back at what has been, or even looking at what is now present, we have to look forwards to discern what it is that is required for the purpose, the *intent*, of the Universe to be fulfilled, of Love to be fulfilled. Perhaps, then, and here I repeat myself, the answer to the question is that if Love is seeking to re-unite with Love through the evolution of Love, then Love must require that we *learn to love*, ever more to develop our capacity to love, or as Teilhard asserts, that we reach out towards higher and higher levels of Loving Consciousness.

In his book *The New Cosmic Story*,[131] this is what Professor John Haught, himself a 'student' of Teilhard, calls Anticipation, "an anticipatory vision of the universe", which:

> ...looks towards a universal religious meaning arising obscurely on the future horizon of cosmic becoming.[132]

His work considers the role played by religion in the evolution of the unfolding universe. For, in terms of noting the ongoing rise of consciousness, it must surely be recognized that in the arising of religious expression and practice, not least in the Axial Age in the eighth to the third centuries BCE, religion has made a significant contribution:

> Between two thousand and three thousand years ago a shift in human consciousness began to occur on Earth that was so unprecedented that it amounts to nothing less than a major new chapter in the history of the universe.[133]

He goes on to say that over a period of several centuries, especially in China, India, Europe and the Near East:

> ...the religious quest for meaning became less symbolic and more mystical and theoretical than earlier. In the teachings of a few exceptional seekers and their followers, religion in these places became less concerned with rituals, petitions, and appeasement

of supernatural beings and more preoccupied with personal awakening and spiritual transformation.[134]

Indeed, Haught claims that "connecting a scientifically informed cosmic awareness to our spiritual lives was Teilhard's main preoccupation." [135]

> Moreover, what theology had formerly idealized as the primacy of spirit gradually became for Teilhard the primacy of the Future.[136]

"A good name for this Future is 'God',"[137] says Haught, which, as I have made clear earlier, I would, of course, translate as meaning that the name for this Future is 'Love'. And, to some extent at least, Haught agrees when he says:

> Infinite Love is the vital energy of this movement toward a new future of the universe.[138]

But how might this occur? Haught says that Teilhard supposed that in moving from one form of complexity to the next, the universe "passes through three distinct phases: divergence, convergence and emergence."[139] This pattern, he says, is replicated at every stage of cosmogenesis.[140] And in wondering what this 'emergence' might be, he suggests, again following Teilhard, that it would require three qualities: vitality, subjectivity and creativity.[141] Vitality includes the capacity to strive; subjectivity includes an increase in sentience, perceptivity, consciousness and self-awareness; and, in remaining open to the not-yet, creativity fosters:

> the emergence of unprecedented forms of life and the enhancement of vitality, subjectivity, diversity, relationality, and creativity in the up-ahead.[142]

Where, then, are we in this? We are, perhaps, at a point of transition, a transition between a long period of divergence and a coming period of convergence that, should it be attained, would lead to the emergence of a new, and at present unknown, state of higher consciousness, perhaps this will be a state of what I am now calling

'Great Love'.

And so to rephrase what was said earlier, our question, perhaps, should be: What would a future state of Great Love require of us now? How do we enter a nourishing state of convergence in order that, in time, Great Love can emerge? And how can we bring about forms of convergence that do no not stifle creativity and vitality?

In reflecting on this matter of convergence, and indeed upon the whole matter of a universe inclined towards relationships, I have found myself re-reading the early parts of Kenneth Gergen's *Relational Being*,[143] a text to which I referred in Chapter 7 of *The Recovery of Love*.[144] For if universal Love is an inclination towards relationship, then we need to know more about what Gergen calls relational being.

At the outset of his text, Gergen lays out his intent:

> My attempt is to generate an account of human action that can replace the presumption of bounded selves with a vision of relationship. I do not mean relationships between otherwise separate selves, but rather, a process of coordination that precedes the very concept of self.[145]

And:

> This vision of relational being will invite us, then, to set aside the freedom/determinism opposition, and to consider the world in terms of relational confluence.[146]

The matter could not be more clearly stated. The present dogma of separation and conflict is entirely unsuited to what is now needed – a narrative of 'relational confluence'. And the more I read of this in Gergen's work, the more essential it seems to become. For when we look around us at the dire consequences and dangers of a culture of separation governed by a doctrine of 'market value', the more we are bound to ask why it is that we should question Gergen's proposition at all. Surely it must be that it is the task of those who have brought us to where we are, those who promote separation as an unquestioned convention, that should explain themselves. Can they tell us what their fragmented reality is based upon, and where do they think it takes us?

As Gergen himself puts it:

> Why must we unthinkingly sustain a tradition in which the primary site of evaluation is the individual self? Why must the prizing of one's individual mind serve as the essential ingredient of the good life? When we cease to think in terms of bounded beings, we take a step toward freedom from the ratcheting demands of self-worth.[147]

Surely it makes sense to consider some other possibility, what Gergen refers to as "more promising forms of life."[148] In this, I am inclined to urge myself – and any others that will accompany me – to move beyond the so-called rationality of the mind and to *imagine what might be*. For without imagination we are ever locked into the tyranny and boundaries of convention. As Gergen puts it:

> …there are important ways in which the presumption of persons as bounded units now emerges as a threat to the well-being of the world…[149]

He regards his work as:

> [sketching] an alternative to the tradition of bounded being. This vision, relational being, seeks to recognize a world that is not within persons but within their relationships, and that ultimately erases the traditional boundaries of separation.[150]

And so, as I have undertaken this exploration of the arising of Love, I have found that Gergen's text matters, not only because it critiques our dominant culture of separation and conflict, with its heightened expression of the individuation of 'bounded selves', but also because it challenges the prevalent discourse and puts forward an essential discourse of relatingness, a world in which there is only relationship, which for me, of course, means a world in which there is only Love. For if we focus only on the 'bounded self' how can we understand a world of relationships.[151]

How we speak of this matters, and Gergen is helping us to use a language of relationships, that which he calls a relational discourse, a discourse in which we begin to see "that our vocabulary is essentially [and I would say must be] a vocabulary of relationship."[152]

If you read the work of cosmologists you will, of course, find that they use their own language, their own way of describing things. But suppose we spoke with the voice of Love. If we did so, perhaps we might describe the origin of our Universe differently. Just as an example, therefore, in Appendix 1, I offer you a different story of the birth of our Universe. Any errors are entirely mine!

Endnotes

1. Lao-Tzu, *Tao Te Ching: The Book of the Way*, Translated by Stephen Mitchell, Kyle Cathie, 1988, Chapter 25.
2. David Cadman, *Love and the Divine Feminine*, Panacea Books, 2020, 6.
3. David Cadman, *Love and the Divine Feminine*, Panacea Books, 2020, 6.
4. Louis M. Savary and Patricia H. Berne, *Teilhard de Chardin On Love: Evolving Human Relationships,* Paulist Press, 2017; and Louis M. Savary, *Teilhard de Chardin's The Phenomenon of Man Explained*, Paulist Press, 2020.
5. Brian Swimme, *The Universe Is a Green Dragon: A Cosmic Creation Story*, Bear & Company, 2001; and Brian Swimme, *Cosmogenesis: An Unveiling of the Expanding Universe*, Counterpoint, 2022.
6. Jude Currivan, *The Cosmic Hologram: In-formation at the Center of Creation*, Inner Traditions, 2017; and Jude Currivan, The Story of Gaia: *The Big Breath and the Evolutionary Journey of Our Conscious Planet*, Inner Traditions, 2022.
7. The phrase 'Big Bang' was first used by Fredrick Hoyle in 1950.
8. Private conversation 12th April 2023.
9. Louis M. Savary and Patricia H, Berne, *Teilhard de Chardin on Love: Evolving Human Relationships*, Paulist Press, 2017.
10. Ibid. 3.
11. Ibid. 5.
12. Ibid.
13. Ibid. xi quoting 1 John 4:8.
14. Louis M. Savary, *Teilhard de Chardin's 'The Phenomenon of Man' Explained*: Paulist Press, 2020, 15-17
15. Louis M. Savary and Patricia H, Berne, *Teilhard de Chardin on Love: Evolving Human Relationships*, Paulist Press, 2017. ix.

16 Ibid. 19.
17 John F. Haught, *The Cosmic Vision of Teilhard de Chardin*, Orbis Books, 2021, 13.
18 Louis M. Savary and Patricia H, Berne, *Teilhard de Chardin on Love: Evolving Human Relationships*, Paulist Press, 2017, 25.
19 Louis M. Savary, *Teilhard de Chardin's 'The Phenomenon of Man' Explained*: Paulist Press, 2020, 4.
20 Ibid.
21 Pierre Teilhard de Chardin, *Le Phénomènon Humaine*, translated by Sarah Appleton-Weber, Oxford University Press, 1999, 188.
22 Ibid. 189.
23 Ibid. 190.
24 Louis M. Savary, *Teilhard de Chardin's 'The Phenomenon of Man' Explained*, Paulist Press, 2020, 87.
25 Ibid. 7.
26 Ibid.
27 Brian Swimme, *Cosmogenesis: An Unveiling of the Expanding Universe*, Counterpoint, 2022.
28 Ibid.3.
29 Ibid. 4.
30 Ibid. 8.
31 Ibid. 78.
32 Ibid. 81.
33 Ibid. 144.
34 Ibid. 175-176.
35 Ibid. 176.
36 Ibid 183.
37 Ibid. 189.
38 Ibid. 192.
39 Ibid. 194.
40 Ibid. 195.
41 Ibid. 197.
42 Ibid. 207.
43 Ibid. 208.
44 Ibid. 212.
45 Ibid. 217.

46 Ibid, 217-218.
47 Ibid. 226.
48 Ibid. 226.
49 Ibid. 227.
50 Ibid. 235.
51 Ibid. 235-236.
52 Ibid. 246.
53 Ibid. 257.
54 Ibid. 253.
55 Ibid. 254.
56 Ibid. 260.
57 Ibid. 284.
58 Ibid. 290.
59 Ibid. 291.
60 Ibid. 291-292.
61 Ibid. 295.
62 Ibid. 314.
63 Ibid. 315.
64 Brian Swimme, *The Universe Is a Green Dragon*, Bear & Company, 2001.
65 Ibid. 40.
66 Ibid.
67 Ibid. 43.
68 Ibid.
69 Ibid. 57.
70 David Cadman, *The Recovery of Love: Living in a Troubled World*, Zig Publishing, 2020, Chapter 2.
71 Jude Currivan, PhD, *The Cosmic Hologram: In-formation at the Center of Creation*, Inner Traditions, 2017.
72 Ibid. xiv.
73 Private conversation February 2023.
74 Jude Currivan, PhD, *The Cosmic Hologram: In-formation at the Center of Creation*, Inner Traditions, 2017, 181.
75 Ibid.
76 Ibid. 183.
77 Ibid. 191.
78 Ibid.
79 Jude Currivan PhD, *The Story of Gaia: The Big Breath and

	the Evolutionary Journey of Our Conscious Planet, Inner Traditions, 2022.
80	Ibid. 6.
81	Ibid.
82	Ibid. 20-21.
83	Ibid. 23.
84	Ibid. 29.
85	Ibid. 35.
86	Ibid. 48.
87	Ibid.
88	Ibid. 52.
89	Ibid.
90	Ibid. 70.
91	Ibid. 81.
92	Ibid. 93.
93	Ibid. 94.
94	Ibid. 110.
95	Ibid.
96	Ibid. 110-111.
97	Ibid. 111.
98	Ibid. 113-114.
99	Ibid. 158.
100	Ibid. 132.
101	Ibid. 196.
102	Ibid.
103	Ibid.
104	Ibid.
105	Ibid. 198.
106	Ibid.
107	David Cadman, *Love and the Divine Feminine*, Panacea Books, 2020, 6.
108	Jude Currivan PhD, *The Story of Gaia: The Big Breath and the Evolutionary Journey of Our Conscious Planet*, Inner Traditions, 2022, 249.
109	Ibid. 251.
110	Humberto Maturana Romesin and Gerda Verden-Zoller, *The Origin of Humanness*, Edited by Pille Bunnell, Imprint Academic, 2008.

111 Jude Currivan PhD, *The Story of Gaia: The Big Breath and the Evolutionary Journey of Our Conscious Planet*, Inner Traditions, 2022, 263.
112 Ibid. 263-264. The trinity of feminine, masculine attributes with child is explored in Jude Currivan, *The 8th Chakra: What It Is and How It Can Transform Your Life*, Hay House, 2006 and 2012.
113 Private conversation 12th April, 2023.
114 Ibid.
115 Rupert Spira, *The Nature of Consciousness: Essays on the Unity of Mind and Matter*, Sahaja Publications, 2017, 10.
116 Rupert Spira, *The Transparency of Things: Contemplating the Nature of Experience*, Sahaja Publications, 2016, 15.
117 Rupert Spira, *The Nature of Consciousness: Essays on the Unity of Mind and Matter*, Sahaja Publications, 2017, 3.
118 Ibid. 5.
119 This extract comes from a talk given by Rupert Spira at a retreat held in California in March 2022.
120 Rupert Spira, *The Heart of Prayer,* Sahaja Publications, 2023, 17-18.
121 Rupert Spira, *The Transparency of Things: Contemplating the Nature of Experience* Sahaja Publications, 2016, 15.
122 Ibid. 100.
123 Ibid. 111.
124 Rupert Spira, *The Nature of Consciousness: Essays on the Unity of Mind and Matter*, Sahaja Publications, 2017, 31.
125 Ibid. 31-32.
126 Ibid. 33.
127 David Cadman, *Love and the Divine Feminine,* Panacea Books, 2020, 6.
128 Pierre Teilhard de Chardin, *Le Phénomènon Humaine*, translated by Sarah Appleton-Weber, Oxford University Press, 1999, 188.
129 Brian Swimme, *Cosmogenesis: An Unveiling of the Expanding Universe*, Counterpoint, 2022, 78.
130 Ibid. 235.
131 John F. Haught, *the New Cosmic Story: Inside Our Awakening Universe*, Yale University Press, 2017.

132	Ibid. 42.
133	Ibid. 10.
134	Ibid.
135	John F. Haught, *The Cosmic Vision of Teilhard de Chardin*, Orbis Books, 2021, xi.
136	Ibid. 3.
137	Ibid.
138	Ibid. 4.
139	Ibid. 6.
140	Ibid.
141	Ibid. 200-207.
142	205.
143	Kenneth J. Gergen, *Relational Being: Beyond Self and Community*, Oxford University Press, 2009.
144	See Chapter 7 of David Cadman, *The Recovery of Love*, Zig Publishing, 2022.
145	Kenneth J. Gergen, *Relational Being: Beyond Self and Community*, Oxford University Press, 2009, xv.
146	Ibid. xv1.
147	Ibid. 12.
148	Ibid. xxvii.
149	Ibid. 4.
150	Ibid. 5.
151	Ibid. 17.
152	Ibid. 70.

Chapter 2

Mother and Child

The Tao says:

Being full of power
is like being a baby.
Scorpions don't sting,
tigers don't attack,
eagles don't strike.
Soft bones, weak muscles,
but a firm grasp.
Ignorant of the intercourse
of a man and woman
yet the baby penis is erect.
True and perfect energy!
All day long screaming and crying,
but never hoarse.
True and perfect harmony.[1]

Love said:

"True being arises, can only arise, from Being in Love – Great Love, divine, universal, eternal, without time and dimension, within all that is. For I am the motion, the flux, the pulse of all that is.

"Being in love, you are united with being in Love. Without this you are separated and cannot see nor speak of anything that is true. To find Truth, find me – be in love, Be in Love. To rest and be at peace, dwell in me – be in love, Be in Love."[2]

In moving from the universal to the personal, we now come to another birthing, the birthing of a child, an exploration of the relationship between the mother and child and the arising of love between them in utero and when the child is newborn, the first weeks and months of the child being born. The relationship between mother and child is one of those primal relationships in which Love is assumed to be present, or at least is expected and hoped for, and my reflection is based upon a review of the scientific literature of what is happening neurologically, biologically and to some extent psychologically at this time, prepared by my research assistant Antonia Gergen and supervised by my colleague Dr. Vikki Lee (see Appendix 2). It starts with what is happening for and to the child, and then what is happening for and to the mother.

Here, in this chapter, I seek to place the research within the context of my primary thesis on Love – that Love is of the essence, seeking to find another answer to the question of what it is that Love requires in order to become manifest. As will become clear, what we have discovered, or at least what I shall claim has been discovered, is that we are born to love and that we are then intentionally held in Love.

As my colleague, Vikki, has explained to me, throughout the twentieth century key theories emerged in the psychological literature to explain the connection-seeking behaviours of infants to their primary care-giver. From Freud's drive theory to Bowlby's theory of attachment, these theories sought to describe the process of human bonding through psychological explanations. In the twenty-first century, evidence for, and occasionally against, these theoretical models has been presented at the neurological level. In addition, the scientific techniques now available to investigate neural activity have enabled new theories, such as polyvagal theory, – the role of the vagus nerve in emotion regulation, social connection and fear response – to emerge.

I am most grateful to Vikki and Antonia for their work. All the errors of interpretation are mine.

The review of the literature of the relationship between the mother and her child in utero and when the child is newborn (as set out in Appendix 2) describes the ways in which there is an ongoing and physical interweaving of giving and receiving. For example, in the mother's protection of the child from cortisol stress and the sharing of the comfort of oxytocin, it seems evident that the child is intended to be born into a bonded relationship with her mother. What is more, it seems that even if this bond is for survival, it is not primarily and only for food but, most importantly, it is in order to love and be loved. Indeed, we might say that *survival requires Love*. The words 'pleasure' and 'comfort' that the scientists use, and to which are referred in the literature review, imply, but may not adequately describe, this deeply bonded relationship, that which I would call a *loving relationship*.

It seems that for Love to arise, the physical being of the child has to be such that she naturally 'turns to' her mother, and that she can discern the presence of her mother in such a way that her mother is 'known'. It would seem, for example, that the working of the nervous system, through 'white matter density', is quite specifically shaped for this purpose. Furthermore, as I have said, the mitigation of cortisol, and the production and sharing of oxytocin within the relationship of mother and child, would seem to be for the specific purpose of maintaining a sense of loving union, a secure sense of being loved and giving love. If, for whatever reason, the first is not mitigated and the second is not shared, it is said that the child will suffer both in the short and the longer term. This regulation is part of a natural internal and shared happening, and would seem to be how the mother and the child are meant to be. Thus, we can say that the development of a loving relationship is deliberate and intended.

I suggest that this implies that for Love to arise there must be what Teilhard de Chardin described (see Chapter 1 above) as the first two stages of an evolution of Love – Attraction and Connection. Both the mother and her child are intended to be attracted to each other and then connected to each other. Indeed, to take Teilhard's evolutionary law on to its fourfold completion, their coming together gives rise to new Complexity in the being of the child, with the potential for higher and higher levels on Consciousness. For Love to arise, then, it would seem that there must be a capacity and a willingness both to receive and to give love. And if this is true for the mother and her child, then, as we have begun to see, it is part of the wider evolutionary law of Love. As adults we may need to learn to love, but we can now see that we may well have already known this in utero and in the neonatal state. Perhaps we should say that we must re-learn to love.

Although it is not clear from the review of the literature quite when Love arises between mother and child, the fact that it is intended would seem to be unquestionable. And it would seem that the purpose of these happenings is of as much importance, if not more so, than the response to hunger in the child. One might almost say that the child appears to need love more than food. No doubt she needs both.

The process of myelination, also seems to be designed specifically, to support a bonded relationship, without which the child does not prosper. The review says:

> The myelination of the cranial nerve begins during the fifth foetal month, and continues until a child reaches 24 months in age. In this crucial time window, bidirectional communication with the mother either advances or impedes myelination processes throughout the nervous system, shaping the individual baseline heart rate. [3]

Again, in the literature review, I note that 'the science' suggests that consciousness does not appear in the foetus until some 24-25 weeks of pregnancy. This view would seem to be based upon the fact that, at present, it has not been possible to measure a pain or pleasure response before that time. Accepting, of course, that I have no scientific basis for doing so, but also noting that some of the literature is suggesting earlier signals of consciousness, I wonder whether the lack of measurement is a sufficient reason for coming to this 24-25 week conclusion. If, as we saw in Chapter 1, consciousness is present in all that is, and is certainly present within the cells of the human body, then consciousness would be present in the foetus, whether or not it is entirely a separate part of the mother's body. If this is so, then it would seem that we can only say that we do not yet have a way of observing this. Perhaps we might also suggest that the evident and early response of the child to the mother might go some way to explaining the experience of unity or 'union with' that some psychologists refer to as being significantly embedded in all of us. Might it be that the foetus, and then the unborn child, is aware and conscious from the very beginning?

However that may be, one of the interesting findings of the review is that the new born baby is extra-specially designed for bonding, having significantly more potential bonding neurons in the brain than will be the case later in life. As we say:

> An infant's brain holds approximately 100 billion neurons – 15 per cent more than the developed adult brain. Evolutionarily, the significance of this excessive neural capacity is to facilitate specific learning processes, social bonding, and language acquisition. As early schemas become more established and assimilated into neonate consciousness, unused neuronal connections are eliminated for functional efficiency in a process called synaptic pruning.[4]

As an aside, in all of these respects, I refer to the work of my colleague, Jackie Sussman,[5] and her Inner Vision Group in America. She has shared with me a report of an inner-visioning session in which the women in this group, of which all but one had given birth, were led to imagine and then describe the period of the child in the womb and at birth. All envisioned their pregnancy as being characterised as a period of loving calm, as if everything was as it should be, whilst their memories of childbirth were of a time that was much more painful and, in some cases, frightening, suggesting that the physical separation of child from mother is likely to be shocking for both the mother and the child.

The review affirms this when it says:

> Kasser et al. ... note that coming into life is often painful for a child. During the 4-8 hours of average active labour, the newborn is woken up and physically alerted by contractions and elevated stress levels in the mother, which in turn trigger noxious-evoked brain activity and make the child more receptive to any incoming sensory information. Both vaginal and caesarean births place pressure on the young nervous system, and orient consciousness to prioritize survival needs.[6]

Firstly, in utero and during the neonatal phase, the mother undergoes a number of neurological and biological changes. For example, the review says that Hoekzema suggests that:

> ...these functional changes are common across mammalian

species ... Like most adaptations do, the reallocation of mental resources serves as an important evolutionary function: it braces the maternal system to protect and feel attached to her offspring.[7]

In the third trimester, the mother experiences an increased activity in 'the default-mode network', which brings her attention inward to a manner of being that is sometimes called having a 'mommy brain'. In other words, the mother is beginning to focus her attention increasingly on the needs of the child, fuelling the parent-to-infant bond. A nesting instinct is arising in the mother to, as we say, ensure a safe environment for the newborn. In this, we conclude as follows:

> ... the emerging feelings of attachment during pregnancy appear to be dependent on neural changes that allow the mother to form a mental image of the foetus. Her willingness to nurture the baby is rooted in the quality of this image, along with the phenomenological experience of differentiation between herself and the baby.[8]

As my colleagues point out, most of these changes are driven by the hormonal and neurotransmitter fluctuations that occur throughout gestation. Progesterone supplementation is seen to increase the activity rate in the mother's reward system, facilitating the formation of maternal bonding by enhancing feelings of satisfaction in the dopamine circuits, and heightening the expression of oxytocin receptors that promote maternal bonding. Progesterone is also reducing the activity of the prefrontal cortex, again focussing the mother's attention on her child. At the same time, an absence of adequate levels of oxytocin and increased levels of cortisol, may arise from, and give rise to, harmful levels of stress in both the mother and the child, corroding the spontaneous emergence of affection during pregnancy, primarily through intervening with regulatory mechanism in the placenta.

Coming to the placenta brings us to what I, having no scientific training, regard as wondrous. This is what my colleagues have referred to as the mother-foetus dyad, the relationship that I would call *the loving relationship, between the mother and the unborn child:*

> ...most processes within the mother-foetus dyad operate with a level of synchrony or co-dependence. In fact, the relationship between a mother and her unborn child is sometimes considered biologically mutualistic. Mutualism refers to a form of symbiosis where both organisms benefit from each other's presence.... Hormonal transmission marks the first example of symbiosis, whereby maternal affection toward the child is initiated by placental activity.[9]

The placenta becomes the primary conduit for shared experience and change, unique in that it consists of both maternal blood cells and foetal cells, 'feeding' the child and removing wastes back into the mother's bloodstream. Again, as my colleagues say:

> Most of the oxygen that allows the foetus to 'breathe' in utero flows directly into its heart, revealing that the heart and the lungs are the prenatal locus of life in co-inhabitation.[10]

This remarkable and wondrous 'dance' synchronises the heartbeat of mother and child, the foetus sensing the rhythmic shifts in the mother's breath and adapting its own heartbeat accordingly, its nervous system being highly sensitive to its mother's levels of stress.

The protective powers are bidirectional. Whilst the mother is preparing her child for life outside the womb, the child plays a role in maintaining her mother's health. The review refers to the work of Keelin O'Donoghue,[11] who describes a process in which:

> ...a small amount of foetal stem cells travel through the placenta into the mother's bloodstream, and subsequently assist in tissue repair during and after pregnancy. Animal and human studies on foetal microchimerism suggest that foetal stem cells may have naturally pathogenic and reparative qualities, making them an agent of maternal immunological wellbeing. This hypothesis is supported by the finding that microchimeric cells inhabit the mother's bone marrow and organs for decades after giving birth.[12]

Then we come to birth, which is an exceptionally neurologically active time for the maternal system, a time in which both mother and child mutually participate:

> Once sufficient foetal maturation has occurred, the baby's lungs begin to secrete small amounts of surfactant protein into the mother's bloodstream. These proteins act as a chemical signal that the foetus is ready to breathe outside the womb. As a response, the mother's body begins to release large amounts of reproductive hormones that initiate and regulate the labour process. By recognising the active roles of both mother and child in birth, we create a synergistic birth narrative.[13]

Once again rising levels of oxytocin play a part, softening the cervix and initiating contractions, creating a safe passageway for the baby whilst at the same time lowering the mother's stress levels both during and after labour. As if to help, most of the oxytocin is the result of the baby's head pressing against the cervical wall. And, indeed, the unborn child itself produces small amounts of oxytocin in the moments before birth. As is recorded in the review:

> This simultaneous oxytocin release is one of the most fascinating markers of neurological synchrony between the mother and her child. It supports the idea that childbirth is a process of dyadic synergy.[14]

Indeed, I note that this matter of synergy or mutualism, or *loving relatedness* as I would call it, keeps coming up in the literature review. In responding, I have used the words, 'wondrous' and 'fascinating', because theses words describe this remarkable *mutuality in utero*. During pregnancy the pituitary glands release into the bloodstream natural opiates, beta-endorphins, that alleviate some pain and stress for the mother, thereby strengthening the bond between mother and child. These beta-endorphins are also released during breastfeeding, and their prolonged release suggests the mother-child bond is not realised in an instance but by a sustained positive neural feedback. Interestingly, some suggest that the modern use of analgesics may impair the production of natural pain reduction as part of what has been called 'birthing consciousness'.

Finally, once the mother has given birth to her child, further change occurs. In the few weeks leading up to birth and up to two years after, the grey matter decrease from early pregnancy begins to slowly reverse itself, the re-expansion of brain matter reflecting the emergence of new neural connections that support bonding and memory formation. And the mother's brain never returns to how it was before motherhood. As it has been put it in the review:

> It is as if the prenatally acquired vigilance is finally put into action to assure bonding in postnatal separation. The mother's efficient learning abilities and responsiveness ultimately contribute to a long-lasting bond with the child and assure mutual wellbeing.[15]

Rather than a random outcome, what we are seeing here is an intended process. The mitigation of cortisol, the production of oxytocin and of white matter and myelination, are all intended to enable the newly born child to bond with her mother. They are all inclined to ensure that the child seeks relationship. With Teilhard de Chardin in mind, one might say that both the mother and the child are 'designed' for a necessary and intended outcome that is required by the impulse of Love, through Love to Love, to make possible higher and higher levels of loving Consciousness. Love is the energetic force that brings together – Attraction and Connection continue with Complexity and Consciousness.

What then does this tell us of Love and of the conditions that are necessary for the arising of Love? Surely it is that we are born with the intention, almost the requirement, to love and be loved; that our bodies and minds are 'wired' to facilitate this process. And so this chapter takes its place alongside Chapter 1. If it is that Love is of the essence, that our unfolding Universe is Love flowing from Love to Love – perhaps Love flowing from Original Love to Great Love – then it is hardly surprising that our birth and life is intended to play its part in this; that our physiology and neurology is intended to help this happen; that mother and child co-create loving being.

Endnotes

1. Lao-Tzu, Tao Te Ching: *A Book About The Way and the Power of the Way*, translated by Ursula K. Le Guin, Shambala, 1998, Chapter 55.
2. David Cadman, *Love and the Divine Feminine*, Panacea Books, 2020, 6.
3. Appendix 2, page 115.
4. Appendix 2, page 119.
5. Private correspondence with Jacki Sussman, January, 2023.
6. Appendix 2, page 118.
7. Appendix 2, page 121.
8. Appendix 2, page 122.
9. Appendix 2, page 124.
10. Appendix 2, page 124.
11. Appendix 2, page 125.
12. Ibid.
13. Appendix 2, page 127.
14. Appendix 2, page 128.
15. Appendix 2, page 130.

CHAPTER 3

Reflections:

WHAT DOES GREAT LOVE REQUIRE?

The Tao says:

Heaven will last,
earth will endure.
How can they last so long?
They don't exist for themselves
and so can go on and on.

So wise souls
leaving self behind
move forward,
and setting self aside
stay centred.
Why let the self go?
To keep what the soul needs.[1]

Love said:

"Great Love is an old and lost language. And in your time, being little understood, it is difficult to speak of. Yet without Great Love nothing can be truly understood or said.

"In your disconnected world, you need to know this. Separated and apart, you find no place for me. Seeking only to have and then to have more, you find no place for me. But without me, everything disintegrates and cannot be reunited with the One.

"Whilst you may sometimes see me and feel me in yourselves and in others, it is usually no more than a glimpse, a touch. For Great Love is something other, something beyond and within all that is. Frail as you are, you cannot look upon me directly. And yet, without me nothing can truly be.

"Despite the difficulty, you must do your best to discern my motion. To do otherwise would be to live falsely and proceed in ignorance."[2]

Before beginning to reflect on what might have been learnt from these enquiries into the place of Love in our Universe and Love's arising between mother and child, I have to make one or two things clear.

Firstly, this enquiry has been about, and seen through the lens of, humanity. It does not explore explicitly what can be learnt from enquiries that would include the wider domain of other beings, plants and animals, fungi and trees, bacteria and other forms of life, let alone that which is often regarded as beyond what we have come to call 'being', the rocks, the mountains, the rivers and the oceans. This is not to say that the exploration of what Love needs should exclude any of this – indeed, I would encourage explorations of all of it – but it is to say that I have only been exploring one part of it: humanity's relationship with Love. I accept that we are one with all that is, but, at least for the moment, I have restricted myself to the human realm, albeit that in so doing I have inevitably encountered what might be called the 'edges' of other realms.

It has also been suggested to me that even to speak of 'Love' is to be overly anthropocentric. If that is so, I hope I have shown that the Love of which I am trying to speak precedes all that now is, including us. We cannot suggest that we have exclusive ownership of Love. Indeed, Love and Consciousness are not ours to claim. We, and all that is, are part of a single Love and a single Consciousness. And in this, we should not assume that we, humanity, are somehow at the peak of some kind of evolutionary scale. Who knows? Not me.

Nevertheless, there is a need for us to explore what it is to be truly human in relation to a Universe that is unfolding towards higher and higher levels of Consciousness and Love. Therefore, however small and insignificant it might be, I hope that what I have offered here is a step towards 'Great Love', for as we have seen in the Preface to this text, and at the beginning of this chapter, Love said:

> Whilst you may sometimes see me and feel me in yourselves and in others, it is usually no more than a glimpse, a touch. For Great

Love is something other, something beyond and within all that is. Frail as you are, you cannot look upon me directly. And yet, without me nothing can truly be.

What is certain is that I conclude that Love is a force that is inclined towards right relationship as a whole, and towards particular relationships in the many divergent ways of being. And to summarise, I would say that in all that I have explored I have found an affirmation of my long-held proposition that *'Love is of the essence'*. The explorations behind this text have added to this that Love is an essential part of our birthing, and an essential part of an unfolding Universe intent on moving towards higher and higher levels of consciousness. Linking Love to pure Consciousness, this text has also suggested that we are being drawn forward by the intention of our Universe, *the intention of Great Love*. In all of this, the matter of 'intention' is of great importance, since it is the nature and quality of our intention that matters. Intention can be good or bad, healing or harmful, and the intention that matters is always the former, it is always that which is loving. Finally, I have found in the teachings of the Tao a way of 'seeing' and 'knowing' that shows *Love as being part of an ever-moving coming to be and ceasing to be*, a Love that cannot be defined but only experienced. According to the Tao, what Love requires is nourishment and care, comforting and protecting. It requires that us to be *at ease and full of compassion* (see Appendix 3).

What then does Love require? Overall, it seems to me that it is that we *learn to love*; that we shift our way of knowing so that we can become *ready for Love*; and that we do this so that Being in Love *becomes our habit*. Love in its many manifestations must become our sole way of being – loving kindness, compassion, a care for others and for the Earth. No more and no less. And this requires both *intention* and *humility*. All that we say and do must be said and done in the manner of Love and in a reality of ever-present relatedness.

I also see that coming to this will be helped by the regular practice of Humble Silence, a form of solitary or gathered silence in which we wait, without expectation, for Love to arise within us and beyond us.

These quotes from Kenneth Gergen affirm the need for

relatedness:

[It] is through collaborative action that all meaning emerges.[3]

And:

My hope is to recast the discourse of mind in such a way that human connection replaces separation as the fundamental reality.[4]

For whilst the individualist tradition "continues unfalteringly,"[5]

[we are] immersed in conventions of coordination, and to remove oneself from such conventions altogether is to cease making sense.[6]

I return to the words of Love spoken to me in my study:

Invite me in, and for a while suppose that what I say is true.

And then, later, Love said:

True being arises, can only arise from Love…For I am the motion the flux, the pulse of all that is.

Being in love, you are united with being in Love. Without this you are separated and cannot speak of anything that is true.

So, for me, this seems to say that our intended becoming is: that we hear Love and are guided by Love, in the practise of humility and waiting. I know that we may not be there all the time, that too often we will remain in separation and conflict, and sometimes wonder whether there can be anything else. But learning to suppose another way of being releases our imagination to explore what may become possible. By supposing we can step out of our bounded being for a moment, to leave behind a culture of constraint and domination, makes a space for Love to arise.

Today, Friday 24th March 2023, I woke with a deep feeling of sadness. I could not tell what it was. But then I knew that I was feeling the sadness of Love. When, and if, we become distant from Love, on our own or with others, when we are overwhelmed by the ways in which our being is torn from Love in separation, then sadness will always be there. And sometimes, when we open our heart to Love we are bound to feel the pain and sorrow more acutely than is usual. Love and Sorrow are sisters and often come to us together each holding the other's hand.

I sit and wait quietly saying to myself, "Be still…and wait…Be still…and wait…" No more or less than that.

A grey sky swept by the wind. Cold wind. Wait and be still. Love will come to you. For Love knows you are there and welcomes the chance to nourish you. How else will Love come to Great Love?

In his book, *The Master and His Emissary*,[7] Iain McGilchrist shows us the way in which a favouring of the left hemisphere of our brain, skilled as it is in abstraction and the identification of the particular, has shaped our way of being in such a way that it no longer serves our true needs but, quite literally leads us astray, overshadowing the right hemisphere of our brain which sees the whole and which, I would say, experiences Love most clearly.

Where do we go to find Truth. As I have said, I started this quest with an odd experience – well odd for me – in which I heard Love speaking. Some years later, and having studied all that I have studied, read all the books I have read, and listened to all the webinars and conversations that I have listened to, I discover that that first 'teaching' has proved to be as good as anything else I have learnt. For some reason, I have felt the need to check what had been said to me by exploring what others have said, and in the end by trying to understand what science has revealed in the birth and life of the Universe and in the relationships between mother and child. Now, it seems to me that what science has said is very much what Love said, only Love said it more sweetly. Quite a lot of what I have studied has been too difficult for me, the words, the concepts so unfamiliar that I have had to struggle to understand them. Indeed, I have to accept that there were parts of all of this that I will never understand. Nevertheless there was enough that I did understand that has now made me more sure footed in my own proposition that *Love is of the essence*, that what Love requires is that we *learn to love*, and that resting in Silence and Stillness, waiting without expectation for Love to come, is an essential part of that understanding.

Given the question, what does Love need in order to become manifest, we have learnt that the birth and life of our Universe is an expression of Love, with intent and purpose ever-moving towards higher and higher levels of consciousness, moving towards a Great Love that is calling us forth to learn to love, to explore those ways in which we can become part of *Love's arising*. We have also discovered that in the arising of Love between a mother and her child, from the very beginning we are born into a loving relationship, one in which we share with our mother the necessary conditions in which love will arise. We have learnt that Love asks us to be prepared for Love's arising, and that we must turn to Love to find Love. And in all of this, we have seen that whilst we may go astray and either not give or not receive Love, Love is always present.

We know that all of this is a challenge to our dominant culture of separation from which Love has been lost, but in my work with the Taoist Master, Master Chuang, I have found a language, a philosophy that speaks about Love's wholeness and connection. In Appendix 3, I share some of that work in an essay titled 'Love and the Tao'. It is here that we find a teaching of relatedness, a relational discourse.

As I write these last paragraphs, I would like to highlight a question that I propose to explore in the next form of my enquiry, which will be titled *Love Arising*. Whilst we have now seen that Love is an intended part of our Universe and deliberately present in that most intimate relationship the relationship between mother and child, we see around us evidence of much that is unloving, much that might trouble our sense of being aligned to Love. And so, I am beginning to wonder if our unfolding and evolving Universe requires some element of imperfection, necessary in order that change may take place. Perhaps perfection was always going to be too static and set. And perhaps there is always (has always been) the possibility that in this necessary condition of movement and flow these elements of imperfection could become heightened, taken too far, sometimes leading to breakdown and collapse.

And then, there is another possibility. It would seem that our innate and positive desire to 'belong', our in-built inclination towards community and tribe, has oftentimes led us to create a sense of 'them' and 'us', and that this has at times led to prejudice and harm. As Rutger Bregman describes in his book, *Human Kind*,[8] our desire to be part of the pack seems to lay us open to persuasion and conditioning, behaving in the group in ways that we would shy away from privately and on our own. So another question would be: What is it that turns us away from Love? And if we can be persuaded to be unloving, what would encourage us to love, and could this become the dominant impulse for humanity on Earth?

As I come to an end, I report that I have been told that scientists from the US and Japan have just proposed a new law of nature that, to me, seems to envisage the kind of 'unfolding' of our Universe that Teilhard de Chardin spoke of and to which I have referred in Chapter 1. These scientists are calling this 'the law of increasing functional information', and apparently it asserts that complex systems evolve towards greater patterning, diversity and complexity. This law, they say, provides a comprehensive framework applicable across various scales, filling gaps left by traditional scientific laws.

It is now October and the light is giving way to the dark, *yin* is receiving the waning energy of *yang*, bringing it into the darkness so that it can be rested, restored and renewed for Springtime. Perhaps this is a good moment to stop writing and to leave the text to be what it is, for whoever may choose to read it...or not!

For those of you who have reached this final paragraph, I thank you for being with me, sharing the path, and for a while supposing that what Love says may be true.[9]

Endnotes

1. Lao-Tzu, Tao Te Ching: *A Book About The Way and the Power of the Way*, translated by Ursula K. Le Guin, Shambala, 1998, Chapter 7.
2. David Cadman, *Love and the Divine Feminine*, Panacea Books, 2020, 8.
3. Kenneth Gergen, *Relational Being: Beyond Self and Community*, Oxford University Press, 53.
4. Ibid. 62.
5. Ibid. 69.
6. Ibid. 74.
7. Iain McGilchrist, *The Master and His Emissary: The Divided Brain and the Making of the Western World*, Yale University Press, first published in 2010 and republished in 2018.
8. Rutger Bregman, *Human Kind: A Hopeful History*, Bloomsbury, 2012, first published in 2020.
9. On the roles of function and selection in evolving systems, *Proceedings of the National Academy of Sciences* (2023). DOI: 10.1073/pnas.2310223120. doi.org/10.1073/pnas.2310223120

Appendix 1:
Another Beginning

In Nowhere, in the time of No Time, and in the place of No Place, there was a coming together. All that was met with all that was. There was a murmuring and ripples of energy sparked across. And then there arose a glowing and a throbbing. There was laughter and sneering. There was compassion and there was stillness. But most of all, there was Silence, a deep and vast Silence, which would have gone on forever had not a Thought arisen. In Nowhere, in the place of No Place and in the time of No Time, you cannot ask from whence a Thought has come. But there it was. And after the laughter and the sneering had gone away, and after all that was was gone, the Thought remained and grew and grew. It swelled up and then, on an impulse, became so small it might have been missed had not an angel been passing by and heard in a whisper the words: "Let us make Love."

And so it was that all that is began to be. Not all at once, of course, not all at once. Indeed, had not an angel been passing by, and had not this angel bent down and cupped the whisper in its hands, and then held it for a while, nothing at all would have happened.

The angel held the whisper to its ear and listened to it again. There it was: "Let us make Love." Then the angel began to wonder and, as we all know, wondering is a wonderful thing.

"If Love is to be made it might need time," the angel said to itself, "and it might need a place to be, and so there must be Time and there must be Place. Where it is now is not at all where it needs to be. It needs a Place of Becoming."

This was a problem because Becoming had not yet been born, but as the angel continued to wonder – and remember wonder is a wonderful thing – Thought came and now whispered into the angel's ear: "Follow me."

The angel and Thought wandered along – although there was really no wandering – until they came to a place that had been forgotten. And in this place was a stream of water, very rare indeed in Nowhere, very rare indeed. It was only there because Thought was thinking about it.

"I wonder," said Thought, to the angel, "I wonder if you were to follow this stream, because I think that if you did, and if you carried the whisper with you most carefully, you might find your way out of Nowhere into a realm of Becoming, a realm that since I have now thought about it might come to be."

"Perhaps that might be so," said the angel.

"But before you go," said Thought, "let me tell the whisper all that I know and all that it will ever need to know."

And so, for a moment, in Deep Silence, and taking the whisper from the angel, Thought shared with the whisper all that it knew and all that the whisper would ever need to know.

Then the angel, now again carrying the whisper most carefully, followed the stream until it had left Nowhere behind.

In Darkness, the angel carried the whisper in its hands and, imagining Time and Place, imagining Somewhere and imagining Becoming, the angel blew upon the whisper the gentlest breath, so that now the whisper Became. And as it became, and in remembering the gentle breath of the angel and all that Thought had told it, the whisper again spoke the words "Let us make Love."

And this was the beginning, and the words that that whisper spoke were offered as a gift, the gift of Love carried in the hands of an angel. It was the vibrational energy of these words, together with all that Thought had said, that caused what we now say was a precise and finely attuned Beginning.

In that very moment, there began the strangest story ever told, a story that we would think was a very long time, fourteen billion years long, but which in Nowhere would have been no time at all. At the very beginning, all that Thought had told the whisper, miraculously began to take form in a place of Somewhere, a realm of Time and Place. But, even at the Beginning, what was to happen did not happen all at once. Indeed, the words that whisper had spoken, "Let us Make Love," were now so powerful that in the first moments of

Somewhere there was such an intensity and such a great heat that nothing else could be. Then, over what for us would again have been a very, very long time, and for our Universe was just a moment, there came a cooling, and in that cooling the first things that ever were Became. And in that time and in the very, very long time that was to come, the one Thought that had in-formed the beginning of our Universe became many thoughts, and then an almost infinitely large number of thoughts. As the ancient wisdom of The Tao tells us: "In the beginning was the one, the one became two, the two became three – and from the three, ten thousand things were born."

To tell the story briefly, at first there were five emergent phenomena, what we now refer to as: energy, matter, space, time and temperature woven into a fabric by the speed of light. These phenomena danced together to co-create forces that would bind and shape our Universe for ever. It would take nearly 400,000 years for the cooling and expanding Universe to bring Light into Being. But there was always a dance and an emergence of relationships, circling and coupling, twirling and spinning, again and again and again. And not all of these were fruitful. Perhaps because some small part of the sneering of the realm of Nowhere had slipped into the memory of Thought, and there were many, many possible relationships that failed and died away.

Nevertheless, over what for us would be very long times, relationships, orders and patterns emerged on the long journey towards what would one day be the birth of Gaia, and what would one day be life on Earth. Elements would be drawn together, particles would be drawn together, or one would seek the other, attraction would arise and then connection

And so Love begat life, and it was abundant.

Appendix 2:[1]

The Early Development of Love as Attachment:

A Neurochemical Review

Prepared by Antonia Gergen

Supervised by David Cadman and
Dr. Vikki Lee

1st June 2023

Preface

In this review of literature, I take on the mysteries of affection between mother and child through a neurochemical lens. My aim is to bring together the recent empirical work of neurologists, developmental psychologists, biologists, and obstetricians around the globe to create a cohesive narrative on the emergence of attachment. Starting from the development of the foetal nervous system to the neurological changes that prepare a woman for motherhood, this review may provide informative and thought-provoking insights into dyadic human psychology.

There are many existing narratives about attachment. Sometimes it is referred to as love, a bond, or unique affectionate behaviour. Many of these ideas capture the social significance of attachment, demonstrating its presence in our cultural fabric throughout time. Given this cultural tradition, a space is also opened for a scientific narrative that takes our socially constructed ideas and gives them a biological foundation. By looking at neural networks, axonal matter, and hormonal transactions, we discover a natural inclination toward bonding.

My own position is defined by a question brought forward by my dear research associate, David Cadman from the Guerrand-Hermès Foundation for Peace. He approached me with the question, "what are the biological foundations that enable love to arise". With this question, came the idea that if one is to study love, it should not be of the romantic kind, but rather the kind of unconditional love that characterizes the relation between mother and child. In order to explore the concept of 'love', our collaborative team, including child and educational psychologist Dr. Vikki Lee, turned to the concept of attachment – a term that aligns more harmoniously with the scientific method. The attachment phenomenon in our review is not to be taken as a continuation to attachment theory, nor is it to be equated with bonding. Although the two concepts are epistemologically similar, we distinguish them by recognizing bonding as an affective state and attachment as the biological and behavioural foundation of the mother-infant relationship.[2]

As further preface, it is imperative to acknowledge the diversity of methodologies to be cited in the literature. For example, I reference a handful of studies that have resorted to animal experimentation when researching neurochemical phenomena in pregnancy. Regrettably, the documentation of ethical procedures undertaken by the researchers in these studies is not always transparent or readily accessible. As we synthesize the findings of these investigations, we hope to stimulate continued discussion on the guidelines for ethical conduct in animal research.[3]

Motherhood is an individually and culturally variable experience, and therefore any correlation or causal relation I discuss must be recognized as contextual. The biological systems that contribute to attachment are largely defined by social identities like religious affiliation, socio-economic status, and family systems, meaning there are always environmental confounds at play. My purpose in this review is not to control for these variables but to approach them as neutrally and respectfully as possible.

The Child in Focus

In studying attachment there is no clear line to be drawn between mother and child, or indeed between the dyad and the greater society. However, in terms of neurology, most research carries a primary focus on either the mother or the child. I begin here with research centered on the child and will turn to the mother in the following section.

Building Safety in the Nervous System

A common misconception about neurology is that it takes place solely within the brain. While the brain is a locus for cognitive processes, its functioning runs through the whole corpus primarily through the central nervous system and endocrine system. These biological networks are fundamental to our examination of the bond between mother and child, because of the role they play in regulating emotional and hormonal states. In the first two chapters of this review, we delve into the key biological systems that support foetal life in and outside of the womb.

The human nervous system consists of the central and peripheral nervous systems, the former operating between the brain and spinal cord, and the latter modulating sensory and motor impulses in the rest of the body. The peripheral motor system is further known to accommodate the autonomic nervous system (ANS), which regulates states of arousal through its tight connections with the limbic organs and endocrine glands in the brain. Limbic nerve cells host human emotional processes and survival impulses, and when activated, cascade into the peripheral nerves through the brainstem. The brainstem and its limbic ties are the most metabolically active regions in neurodevelopment, meaning that there is significant capacity for learning in utero and upon entering the world. In fact, these limbic nerve bundles begin developing in synchrony with maternal movements as early as the 11th gestation week. As we shall see, a unique part of attachment is rooted in the perceptual awakening of the foetal nervous system.

Sue Gerhardt (2004) presents the idea that cortisol, the "stress hormone", plays a defining role in the bond between mother and child.[4] In *Why Love Matters*, the British psychotherapist argues that the mitigation of cortisol release in early development is a precondition for secure attachment bonds. Gerhardt argues that in excess, cortisol is "corrosive" to the nervous system and increases the presence of anxious and fearful behavioural tendencies in later life. Maternal stress hormones subject the foetal nervous system to an aversive arousal state that impedes the development of self-regulatory mechanisms and attachment. Such adverse states are not inherently evil but rather function as an adaptive survival mechanism. The emergence of fearful-avoidant, anxious-preoccupied, and dismissive-avoidant attachment styles is connected to the newborn's inability to regulate aversive arousal states. Bowlby's (1988) psychoanalytic view holds that maternal deprivation, or the lack of a consistent maternal response to an infant's stress, can explain the missing regulation abilities in failed attachment bonds. By examining how maternal responsivity fosters healthy regulation in the young nervous system, we may better understand how stability is established in the dyad. Our species' breeding practices have through time relied on allomaternal input from both other caregivers and the prominent cultural system, therefore the neurochemical correlates of adversity can be considered to an extent a product of both personal and cultural factors.[5]

Nervous system regulation and arousal states are associated with amygdalaic communication with the hypothalamic-pituitary-adrenal (HPA) axis, and subsequent releases of cortisol and adrenaline into the bloodstream. When a child experiences distress, the amygdala is the first limbic organ to respond; it sends repeated electrical impulses down the axon to the hypothalamus and pituitary gland, and eventually to the adrenal glands in the kidneys. This circuit elicits a release of cortisol and epinephrine into the bloodstream, where they increase the heart rate, raise blood pressure, and disrupt metabolic function in the foetal body. In humans, this is known as the slow stress response – one of the most fundamental biomarkers of homeostatic imbalance.

A newborn inherently lacks the physical and mental abilities required to regulate the stress response and bring the body back into a balanced state, which explains the importance of co-regulation with the primary caregiver. Sue Gerhardt (2014) argues that infant emotional repertoires consist of the simple feelings of comfort and discomfort. Discomfort mainly originates from evolutionary needs like hunger or thirst that require consistent maternal responsiveness. When the mother responds to the baby's stress, she is not only alleviating the biological need for food, but the biological need for affection. Feeding the child by natural means initiates skin-to-skin contact, allowing for a sensation of comfort from both nourishment and touch. In early psychology, the primal need for affectionate union was shown in studies like Harlow's (1958) monkey study, where socially deprived infant monkeys chose the comfort of a cloth mother, regardless of whether it provided them with food.[6] In Erich Fromm's (1956) words, to an infant, "mother is warmth, mother is food, mother is the euphoric state of satisfaction".[7] In the fulfilment of this need for affection, the parasympathetic nervous system becomes active, allowing for safety and trust to form in the body. As the process of returning to homeostasis through co-regulation is repeated, the nervous system undergoes structural changes that ultimately reflect the established safety in the bond. Parasympathetic activation lowers the heart rate, stabilizes breathing patterns, and draws blood flow into internal organs, constituting the biological foundation for the ability to bond. The nervous system is the primary communication network through which we observe "attachment" because it evolves gradually to contain knowledge of the quality of the attachment bond.

Vagal Pathways to Flourishing

Stephen Porges' (2017) polyvagal theory has been a cornerstone in interpersonal neurobiology, providing insight into how the infant nervous system develops in safe and unsafe environments. Before delving into the role of the vagus nerve in infant-caregiver bonds, it is necessary to examine the process of myelination. Myelin is a fatty lipid tissue that develops around a nerve cell axon as a means of insulating the cell, regulating circuit function, and speeding the transmission of action potentials. It acts as a biological lubricant for inter-cellular communication and occurs more frequently in highly exercised neural circuits. In polyvagal theory, the ventral vagal pathway maintains a calm autonomic state by regulating breathing patterns and down-regulating sympathetic activation. High exposure to toxic stress, on the other hand, activates the dorsal vagal pathway, which commands the body to immobilize as part of the fight-or-flight reaction.[8] Infants with more adverse early childhood experiences (ACEs) are subject to lower baseline vagal activity, reducing their adaptive strength.[9]

American neuroscientist Stephen Porges' early work was centered around heart rate variability, specifically the connection between sustained attention, cognitive effort, and the heartbeat. His early experimental epiphany was that differences in baseline heart rate variability were significant predictors of individuals' cognitive performance, sensitivity levels, and mental resilience: infants with higher variability were adept at regulating arousal states, while individuals with less variability struggled with a persistent stress response. He later discovered that the "pacemaker of the heart" operates differently between infants depending on the amount of environmental stability in the womb and the first year of life. The myelination of the cranial nerve begins during the fifth foetal month and continues until a child reaches 24 months of age. In this crucial time window, bidirectional communication with the mother either advances or impedes myelination processes throughout the nervous system, shaping the baby's baseline heart rate. Environmental factors that could undermine vagal myelination include placental dysfunction, labour complications, infections during pregnancy, and exposure to drugs. In Porges and Furman (2011), maternal distress during pregnancy and up to two months after interfered with the development of the cerebral cortex, autonomic nervous system, and vagal myelin tissue.[10] Because there is robust connectivity between these biological systems, an early injury to any one of these regions undermines the development of the whole network. When there is an excess of distress, the heart and consciousness are first to respond.

From a neuroanatomical perspective, the heart is a sensory organ just like the eyes or the skin, only it receives information from internal myelinated vagal fibres. Vagal fibres serve either cardio-inhibitory or cardio-excitatory function, meaning that they either slow down or speed up the heart rate in response to environmental stimuli. Sufficient levels of vagal myelin support the individual's visceral regulation abilities by increasing vagal tone and pacing the heart rate in stressful situations. Contrarily, lower levels of vagal myelin decrease vagal tone, making it more difficult to calm the heart. Foetal myelin deficiencies and heart rate irregularities factor into early childhood experiences of attachment by directing the child's behavioural responses in the social atmosphere. Creating a safe and calm environment for the foetus in utero is key to assuring that the child has the internal toolkit for self-expression and social engagement.

Sensation in the Womb: The Question of Consciousness

Sensory perception in utero can be seen as the foetus' first access to conscious mental states. Consciousness, according to American philosopher John Searle (2000), refers to one's "inner, qualitative, subjective states, and processes of sentience or awareness", with the added condition that these states be grounded in autobiographical understanding and mental time.[11] Foetal sensations of pain, and reactiveness to external stimuli are indicative of a preliminary consciousness. However, pure reactivity is insufficient to conclude the presence of deeper autobiographical knowledge. Considering cosmologist Brian Swimme's proposition that love is fundamental to the birth of consciousness,[12] it is necessary to further examine the neural underpinnings of foetal consciousness. Although current empirical research has yet to reach a consensus on the neurological correlates of consciousness, many theories have been offered to explain both its biology and phenomenology.

In light of recent findings, the capacity for pain in gestational development emerges at 24-25 weeks.[13] During this time, connections between the peripheral nervous system and the thalamocortical brain regions begin to support the transmission of external sensory signals. Finally, around the third trimester, the neural ability required to distinguish noxious stimuli from non-harmful stimuli develops. This ability is argued to mark the emergence of preliminary conscious thought. At 7 weeks' gestation, the foetus has developed sufficient sensory receptors for nociception. Evidence of these elementary sensations has so far been a guide to foetal anesthesiological and abortion ethics but has yet to meet the criteria for human consciousness. Even the foetal response to pain is classified as unconscious because it does not engage the cortical regions necessary for sophisticated thinking. Finally, around the 18th gestation week, the endocrine system begins to enhance the ability to feel pain. At this time, foetal cortisol and endorphin levels are found to increase in response to prolonged needling of the intrahepatic (IHV) vein, indicating that a proper stress response is taking effect.[14] Furthermore, the stress response occurs independently from the mother's state of arousal, meaning that the biological union of the dyad does not undermine the individuation of foetal consciousness. Despite being dependent on the mother, the 18-month-old foetus shows clear physiological signs of becoming its own sentient entity.

Baars' (2005) global workspace theory argues that widespread neural communication between primary sensory processing areas and pyramidal cells in the cortex is necessary for consciousness.[15] The global workspace takes bottom-up information from localized sensory areas and forms stabilized mental models with the help of cortically distributed top-down processes. Even without visual perception, the foetus may build schemas that contain sound, memories, percepts of time, and knowledge of the maternal presence. Despite its many strengths, certain limitations apply to global workspace theory when applied to foetal consciousness. Firstly, the information held in the global workspace is arbitrarily available to attentional capture, meaning that even if the information was there, the foetus would lack the ability to attend to and manipulate it. Mature executive function in the frontal lobes is required for the agent to consciously direct attention, yet this ability does not develop until 3-5 years of age.[16] Translated into phenomenal consciousness, this means that a foetus' conscious experience most likely consists of momentary realizations of environmental stimuli.

The first markers of foetal consciousness are crucial to our understanding of attachment because they demonstrate that the foundations for emotional bonding are laid down before birth. Evidence of foetal sentience raises questions about how prenatal experiences, such as maternal stress or emotional interactions, may influence the developing attachment system and long-term attachment outcomes.

Exceptional Sensations

Not all sensory stimuli are created equal when it comes to forming a love bond in the womb. During utero existence, the foetus quickly becomes adept at distinguishing signals originating from the mother from less salient stimuli. The biomarkers for these exceptional events also stand out amidst the average flow of consciousness.

In search of emotionally outstanding stimuli, Kisilevsky et al. (2003) measured foetal heart rate (FHR) changes after hearing a passage read by the mother and a passage read by a stranger. The group found that the maternal voice condition increased foetal heart rate by 5 BPM and that the response was sustained for as long as two minutes after the end of the recording. In contrast, they observed an FHR decrease of 4 BPM when foetuses were exposed to an unfamiliar woman's reading of the same passage. In a later study by the same group, it was observed that the foetal ability to differentiate between maternal and strange speech was only present when individual cardiac vagal tone was high, meaning that the effect was concentrated in foetuses with greater arousal regulation abilities.[17]

Evidence suggests that positive exceptional sensations cause an increase in white matter density.[18] White matter, or axonal myelin, is an indicator of a healthy nervous system and a predictor of high-functioning consciousness in infancy. We find that positive experiences and nurturing maternal behaviours during gestation not only support the development of a more durable nervous system, but also contribute to a general readiness for bonding after birth. On the contrary, an excess of noxious stimulation during gestation correlates with decreased white matter density, which can yield complicated neurodevelopmental outcomes and undermine attachment to the caregiver.[19]

Attachment Readiness at Birth

At the onset of neonatal existence, consciousness begins to manifest itself in observable and vibrant behavioural patterns. In the birthing process, the baby is met by a shockwave of novel input in the sensory modalities, including visual (light), auditory, peripheral somatic (touch, air temperature), gustatory, and olfactory stimuli. Within this environmental context, neural synapses begin to grow rapidly. Kasser et al. (2022) note that coming into life is often painful for a child. During the 4-8 hours of average active labour, the newborn is woken up and physically alerted by contractions and elevated stress levels in the mother, which in turn trigger noxious-evoked brain activity and make the child more receptive to any incoming sensory information. Both vaginal and caesarean births place pressure on the young nervous system, and orient consciousness to prioritize survival needs.[20] The process of birth itself marks a physical disruption in the union between mother and child, meaning that the biological need for maternal presence and reciprocity is intensified.

Swedish paediatrician Hugo Lagercrantz's work has significantly influenced the contemporary understanding of neonatal consciousness. Following the global workspace theory, Lagercrantz and Changeux (2010) argue that if sufficient thalamocortical connections have been established in the womb and somatosensory evoked potentials are able to reach the cortex, the infant has developed beyond purely reflexive behaviours.[21] An infant's brain holds approximately 100 billion neurons–Kasser et al more than the developed adult brain.[22] Evolutionarily, the significance of this excessive neural capacity is to facilitate specific learning processes, social bonding, and language acquisition. As early schemas become more established and assimilated into neonate consciousness, unused neuronal connections are eliminated for functional efficiency in a process called synaptic pruning. For example, newborns can differentiate between the phonemes of every single language in the world, but gradually lose this ability as their native language becomes more exercised. [23]

Similar strengthening and pruning processes apply to the practice of attachment as well. Although the number of neurons in the neonate's brain tends to stay invariable, individual differences in white matter density continue to play a role in early childhood bonding behaviours. Feng et al. (2019) used MRI and diffusion tensor imaging to assess the correlation between white matter microstructures and cognitive learning outcomes in full-term infants. The group measured white matter density at 2 weeks of age, and assessed subjects' cognitive and socio-emotional development at 2 years of age using the Bayley Scales of Infant and Toddler Development.[24] One of the main discoveries was that high white matter integrity at birth correlated with increased socio-emotional, cognitive, and language scores in later childhood. To avoid confounds of prenatal maltreatment, Feng's paradigm studied a population of physically and mentally fit mothers from high socioeconomic backgrounds. The observed correlation supports the idea that neural faculties for forming attachment bonds vary between newborns and depend on the quality of intrauterine maternal care.

Neonate Pleasure Seeking

Sue Gerhardt (2014) suggests that neonate consciousness operates following the pleasure principle. The notion of seeking pleasure and avoiding pain can be tied back to early Freudian theory, according to which all infant behaviour is driven by the search for instant gratification and the subsequent dampening of the animalistic needs that inhabit the unconscious mind. Bowlby speaks of a pleasure system in his work too, but traces the roots of infantile motives to instinct rather than unconsciousness.[25] A more biological perspective suggests that the so-called pleasure principle is crucial for survival and supports the required neurotransmission for attachment bonds. According to this theory, neonate consciousness is directed by an innate drive for pleasure, resulting in a rapid classification of painful and pleasurable stimuli in the external world. The pleasure principle has since been revised to replace the term "pleasure" with "companionship" or "caregiver bond", both of which nevertheless involve pleasure hormone activity.[26] Differentiating between pleasure-seeking and attachment orientation requires a further investigation of the role of the endocrine system in bond formation and maintenance.

Oxytocin: A Key to Bonding

Oxytocin is the most salient neuropeptide released during the neonate's evaluation of sensory stimuli. It facilitates arousal states evoked by both painful/frightening and pleasurable feelings. This neurotransmitter plays a key role in mammalian bonding and group psychology and is argued to be the primary initiating chemical agent of the mother-infant tie. For example, the act of breastfeeding stimulates oxytocin release in the hypothalamus in both the newborn and the mother. Dr. Ruth Feldman (2007) from the Simms Mann Institute describes this parent-infant perceptual synchrony, specifically isochronally positive emotions (i.e. the act of breastfeeding), as building blocks of an affectionate bond.[27] The observed pattern is that (1) a drive for bonding motivates behaviour that is met by (2) maternal response, leading to (3.1) satisfaction through oxytocin and (3.2) attachment.

The chemical pathways that support oxytocin release seem to suggest that the Freudian drive theory is inadequate in describing infant behavioural motives. According to the pleasure principle, infant desires would be satisfied upon oxytocin release. However, in Kirsch and Buchholz's review, it is noted that oxytocin circuits are self-intensifying in nature, meaning that any release of oxytocin is followed by a subsequent burst of more oxytocin. This increases the initial drive, instead of dampening it. The authors also address Bowlby's instinct proposition, stating that the mother-infant bond should not be mistaken for an instinct, because it requires neural and hormonal learning processes that are absent in built-in fear responses. For example, human infants are known to respond fearfully to images of snakes upon first encounter, but the phenomenon of distinguishing the primary caregiver from strangers is rooted in in utero sensory learning. In conclusion, connection feeds the birth of more connection, and the neural circuitry behind the cycle is made of neither drive nor instinct, but the self-intensifying nature of oxytocin responses.

The Mother in Focus

Building the Ability to Attach

From the moment of impregnation, a woman's neurological profile begins to alter in preparation for motherhood. A Dutch group of researchers led by Elseline Hoekzema (2016) used magnetic resonance imaging (MRI) on pregnant mothers and found that the main neurological adaptations in pregnancy take place in the frontal lobes and the limbic system.[28] During the third trimester, the number of cell bodies (grey matter) decreases significantly in the frontal brain regions and hippocampus. In neurology, the frontal cortices are seen to facilitate impulse control and high-level executive function, while the hippocampus is responsible for memory function. Instead of attributing the grey matter volume losses to reduced cognitive abilities, Hoekzema et al. conclude that these functional changes are common across mammalian species and signify a prioritization of significant cognitive tasks over insignificant ones. Like most adaptations do, the reallocation of mental resources serves an important evolutionary function: it braces the maternal system to protect and feel attached to her offspring.

After the 3rd trimester, we begin to see changes in the default-mode neural network (DMN), which operates in resting-state cognition as the mind wanders and introspects. More specifically, neural coherence in the DMN was found to increase in pregnant mothers, reflecting a surge in self and other oriented reflective cognition. There are three main ways to explain the default-mode awakening. Firstly, the reductionist interpretation holds that it is simply the "mommy brain" that is becoming activated, as the mother may become more forgetful and absent minded during reflective states. However, Hoekzema et al. (2022) find that a more elaborate explanation is needed. One key finding in their recent longitudinal study was that the increase in resting-state cognition was positively correlated with measures of foetal differentiation in the Prenatal Attachment Inventory (PAI).[29] Foetal differentiation describes a process in which the mother begins to perceive the foetus as a separate self with its own needs, and simultaneously reassesses her own identity as the caregiver.[30] Differentiation fuels the parent-to-infant attachment bond, which Trombetta et al. (2021) define as "consisting of mental representations, fantasies, emotions, and mental capacities necessary to identify another human being". As the mother personifies the foetus, her efforts to gratify the foetus' needs and avoid separation are fortified. Lastly, the behavioural explanation suggests that the introspective shift is a cognitive prerequisite for maternal nesting behaviours. The "nesting instinct" in mammals refers peripartum preparatory behaviours that ensure a safe environment for the newborn. Indeed, Hoekzema et al. found that expecting women with more default-mode coherence were more likely to tend to the home (the "nest") and experience novelty aversion.

To conclude, the emerging feelings of attachment during pregnancy appear to be dependent on neural changes that allow the mother to form a mental image of the foetus. Her willingness to nurture the baby is rooted in the quality of this image, along with the phenomenological experience of differentiation between herself and the baby.

Pregnancy Hormones in Maternal Bonding

Most changes in maternal neurology are driven by hormonal fluctuations that occur throughout gestation. Progesterone and estrogen, which are produced by the ovaries and the placenta, are two critical hormones when it comes to neuroendocrine regulation.

In addition to offering support to the developing baby, they fuel maternal bonding and the development of nurturing behaviours.

Progesterone enhances the brain's reward system, which is involved in processing positive emotions and reinforcing the repetition of behaviours. The mesolimbic dopamine system consists of dopaminergic neurons that facilitate transmission between the ventral tegmental area (VTA) and nucleus accumbens (NAc).[31] When a pleasurable stimulus is present, a release of dopamine excites these neurons, increasing the motivation to re-engage and maintain the sensation. Progesterone is found to modulate dopamine transmission by increasing receptor sensitivity and expression, contributing to heightened reward processing in expectant mothers. This interaction increases positive reinforcement of maternal behaviours and fosters strong maternal attachment.

Estrogen also exerts significant influence over the reward system. While estrogen has little impact on dopamine circuits, it has been found to contribute to the binding and receptor synthesis of oxytocin in both the brain and uterus.[32,33] Out of the two pleasure hormones, oxytocin is more oriented toward social reward, affiliative behaviours, and physical affection. The relationship between estrogen and oxytocin not only promotes labour but may increase the motivation for caregiving and physical proximity to the child throughout pregnancy.

The placenta maintains healthy progesterone levels by releasing human chorionic gonadotropin (hCG) into the maternal bloodstream, signalling to the ovaries to produce the vital hormone and maintain the pregnancy. Most mothers can produce sufficient progesterone naturally, meaning that human biology inherently supports full term pregnancies and maternal bonding. However, some women experience placental dysfunction or deterioration due to reduced hCG levels. The scientific causes of pregnancy loss remain unknown, but evidence suggests that an excess of free radicals in placental tissues may interrupt hCG production. When there is an imbalance in the ratio of antioxidants to free radicals, the body enters a state of oxidative stress, which impacts both the mother and foetus. Oxidative stress can be caused by many factors, including increased cortisol levels and anxiety in the expecting mother.[34] Other reports find that oxidative stress is amplified by bioenvironmental contaminants found in inhalant drugs, air pollution, and surface toxins.[35] Such factors have a disproportionate effect on mothers from low socioeconomic backgrounds, presumably because of their increased exposure to these stressors. Cortisol intervenes with placental hormone production, damaging both the attachment bond and overall foetal health. Elevated maternal stress levels have thus far been found to increase the risks of foetal mortality, low birth weight, and other birth complications.[36]

Symbiotic Living In Utero

Like with the placenta and progesterone, most processes within the mother-foetus dyad operate with a level of synchrony or co-dependence. In fact, the relationship between a mother and her unborn child is sometimes considered biologically mutualist. Mutualism refers to a form of symbiosis where both organisms benefit from each other's presence, unlike cases of parasitism, where a foreign organism feeds on the host. Hormonal transmission marks the first example of symbiosis, whereby maternal affection toward the child is initiated by placental activity.

The placenta is not only an important mediator of hormonal transmission, but the primary organ through which the foetus receives its vital energy. It begins to form onto the uterine wall during the first three months after fertilization. The placenta is unique in that it consists of both maternal blood cells and foetal cells; this composition allows for a smooth delivery of oxygen and nutrients to the foetus, and conversely, the removal of carbon-dioxide and waste from the foetus back into the mother's bloodstream. Most of the oxygen that allows the foetus to "breathe" in utero flows directly into its heart, revealing that the heart and lungs are the prenatal locus of life in co-inhabitation.

It has also been observed, that the heartbeats of the mother and foetus can synchronize. Dr. P. Van Leeuwen from the University of Aberdeen discovered that maternal breathing patterns impact the foetal heartbeat. By measuring heart-rate synchrony with magnetocardiography, Van Leeuwen et al. (2009) revealed that the foetus senses rhythmic shifts in the mother's breath and adapts its own heartbeat accordingly.[37] Higher maternal respiratory rates–i.e., fast-paced breaths—were associated with the strongest response in the foetal cardiac system. The evolutionary purpose of cardiac synchrony seems to lead us back to Porges' (2017) polyvagal theory. During early and mid-gestation, the foetal nervous system is highly malleable and particularly sensitive to shifts in the mother's stress levels. Cardiac synchrony in high-stress environments that induce rapid breathing negatively impact the vagus nerve, while slower paced breaths foster healthy regulation abilities. One purpose of heartbeat synchrony is then to prepare the foetal nervous system for threatening situations after birth.

The protective powers of the dyad are bidirectional. While the maternal system equips the foetal nervous system for life outside the womb, the foetus plays a role in maintaining the pregnant mother's health. Clinical Obstetrics scholar Keelin O'Donoghue (2008) describes a process in which a small amount of foetal stem cells travels through the placenta into the mother's bloodstream, and subsequently assist in tissue repair during and after pregnancy.[38] The cooperation hypothesis regarding microchimerism, suggests that foetal stem cells have naturally pathogenic and reparative qualities, making them an agent of maternal immunological well-being. After birth, chimeric cells may support maternal caring for the child by manipulating lactation and attachment systems.[39] However, the detection of chimeric cells in wound sites and broken tissues has given rise to the alternate hypothesis that these cells can be damaging and inflammatory. There is more evidence to support the cooperation hypothesis, mainly because mutual survival is in the better interest of both organisms.

It must be noted that there exists some genetic conflict between the mother and child. David Haig (2019) notes that there is a certain evolutionary trade-off that happens in pregnancy, one that favours maternal reproductive health over the health of a particular foetus.[40] According to Haig, the physiological emphasis is on quantity and not quality of offspring, leading to situations where certain biological changes in the mother have little effect on foetal health. For example, human placental lactogen (hPL) is known to mediate maternal metabolism to assure foetal access to sufficient energy and nutrients.[41] However, a handful of case studies showcase successful births despite foetal deletion of hPL genes, implying that the hormone supports primarily the expecting mother's wellbeing.[42] Haig's insight into co-inhabitation does not negate the evident synchrony between the mother and foetus, but rather highlights that it is in the very nature of an organism to prioritize its own survival needs. Attachment, despite being rooted in genealogy, is a more sophisticated process that relies on a combination of psychological, neurochemical, and cultural variables.

Maternal Vigilance

There are many cultural distortions surrounding the concept of the mother's instinct; art, literature, and media throughout times have carefully curated an image of the perfect mother who instinctually knows how to respond to her child's every need. When delving into the biological changes that equip the maternal nervous system for caregiving, it is more helpful and appropriate to avoid the term instinct, and refer to maternal vigilance instead. Vigilance seems a more fitting term, as it captures the various forms of psychological "readiness-potential" that emerge in the mother.

The first instance of vigilance manifests as increased perceptual accuracy. Studies in female rodents show that during pregnancy, a mother's visual, auditory, and olfactory systems become more sensitive to external stimuli. Neuroscientist Craig Kinsley (2014) demonstrated that on average, pregnant rats were five times faster at capturing prey due to improvements to their vision.[43] When the expecting mother processes environmental stimuli more efficiently, her abilities to respond to potentially threatening stimuli are increased. She is able to protect herself and her foetus from harm, increasing the dyad's likelihood of survival. Furthermore, enhancements to sensory processing make her a better huntress when it comes to foraging adequate nourishment during pregnancy. Kinsley reasons that the sensory adaptations in pregnancy are a matter of biological profitability; however, they appear equally supportive of an emerging emotional bond.

Indeed, an expecting mother's emotional vigilance is found to heighten during pregnancy. Between the 17th and 36th gestation week, her abilities to recognize others' emotions through facial affect are improved.[44] From Byrne et al. (2019), we learn that during this time, pregnant women are faster and more accurate at recognizing happy adult faces. This processing advantage is known as the "happy face bias", as it does not seem to apply to sad adult faces or children's faces. Due to its concise scope, the antenatal happy face bias supports the formation of positive emotional bonds during pregnancy. It encourages stronger bonds in the social in-group, which in turn morph into a support network for the mother during her pregnancy.

Although the processing advantage applies mainly to adult faces, it can play a role in healthy foetal-maternal attachment. As a continuation of Byrne's (2019) findings, a Japanese research group led by Takubo Youji (2022) studied facial emotion recognition in mothers who experienced antenatal bonding failures (i.e., struggles in bonding with the unborn child).[45] The group assessed pregnant women (15-28 gestation week) on the Edinburgh Postnatal Depression Scale (EPDS) and Mother-to-Infant Bonding Questionnaire (MIBQ) and accompanied these measures with a facial affect recognition test. The group found that mothers who did not show happy face bias experienced more bonding failures and peripartum depression. These individuals were more likely to rate facial expressions as disengaged. From Youji's findings, we conclude that vigilance is adaptive to an extent. In healthy amounts, it supports maternal social engagement and bonding. However, there are risks of entering the territory of hypo- or hyper-vigilance, where expressions seem completely meaningless or threatening.[46] Vigilance and stress are closely related, and as discussed, prenatal stress (PNS) comes with both benefits and disadvantages.

Birth: Dyadic Synergy

Birth is an exceptionally active time neurologically for the maternal system. Apart from requiring significant biological and psychological efforts from the mother, it requires active agency from the foetus as well. A full-term pregnancy lasts between 37 and 42 weeks, during which ideally the mother has built biological readiness to care for her child, and the child has built biological systems to sustain life outside the womb.[47] Once sufficient foetal maturation has occurred, the baby's lungs begin to secrete small amounts of surfactant protein into the mother's bloodstream.[48] These proteins act as a chemical signal that the foetus is ready to breathe outside of the womb. As a response, the mother's body begins to release large amounts of reproductive hormones that initiate and regulate the labour process. By recognizing the active roles of both mother and child in birth, we create a synergistic birth narrative.

One of the key reproductive hormones involved in labour is the bonding hormone oxytocin. Rising oxytocin levels at the onset of parturition soften the cervix and initiate contractions, creating a safe passageway for the baby. On top of its biological contribution, oxytocin has the psychological impact of lowering the mother's pain and stress levels during labour. Most of the oxytocin produced in labour is the result of the baby's head pressing against the cervical wall.[49] Nerve impulses from the internal pressure then travel to the limbic system and signal the pituitary gland to release oxytocin into the bloodstream. The foetus itself also produces small amounts of oxytocin in the moments preceding its expulsion. This simultaneous oxytocin release is one of the most fascinating markers of neurological synchrony between the mother and her child. It supports the idea that childbirth is a process of dyadic synergy.

During labour, the pituitary gland also releases beta-endorphins into the bloodstream. Beta-endorphins are natural opiates that alleviate pain and stress by inhibiting transmission in synaptic pain receptors.[50] In the central nervous system, beta-endorphins promote pleasurable dopamine transmission. Due to the morphine-like effects of these neuropeptides, labour can feel exciting and rewarding to the mother, strengthening the bond between her and the child. The effects of beta-endorphins are not limited to birth itself, as they are released during breastfeeding as well. The prolonged release of pleasure hormones indicates that the mother-foetus bond is not formed in an instant, but rather bound to sustained positive feedback in the nervous system.

The psycho-phenomenological attributes of labour are equally as focal to our research as the neurochemical ones. Childbirth is a remarkably painful experience, yet mothers throughout time have given birth successfully without the assistance of modern pain medications. Dr. Orli Dahan (2020), head of the Tel-Hai College Consciousness Studies programme has observed in her thorough research an altered state of consciousness during labour.[51] "Birthing consciousness", according to Dahan, is an adaptive mental state that occurs in natural childbirth. Birthing consciousness has the effect of reducing the mother's sensation of pain and increasing her focus during contractions. It also distorts the perception of time and gives rise to feelings of peace and tranquillity after birth. This hypnotic state protects the nervous system from overstimulation and thereby allows for continuity in the attachment bond between mother and child. Dahan proposes that birthing consciousness is explained by transient hypofrontality, which refers to a brief moment during which frontal cortical activity is suppressed. The inhibition of fronto-cortical neurons enhances the effects of deeper limbic cognition (the more primal regions of the brain), and suppresses reflective and executive cognitive processes. The pre-frontal cortex is also seen to play a role in pain processing, which may partly explain the natural pain reduction in birthing consciousness.[52] In recent years, the increasing popularity of modern medical interventions in labour poses a challenge to birthing consciousness. The use of morphine, fentanyl, meperidine, and oxytocin supplements in childbirth could interfere with the natural onset of birthing consciousness. For example, in an observational study, Costa-Martins et al. (2014) found that mothers who reported lower analgesic consumption during labour felt more attached to their babies.[53] Insecurely attached mothers, on the other hand, were more likely to report higher labour pains and use of epidural analgesia. Whether this impact on attachment is associated with the medical intervention itself or difference in individual pain tolerance remains a topic for further study.

Reverberations after Birth

Once the mother has given birth to her child, her neural pathways continue to adapt to motherhood at a fast pace. In the few weeks leading up to birth and up to two years after, the grey matter decrease from early pregnancy begins to slowly reverse itself. This re-expansion of brain matter reflects the emergence of new neural connections that support bonding and memory formation. As the mother holds her new baby and responds to its bids for connection, her brain directs its energy to building neurons from neural stem-cells alongside her child who is also taking in a world of new stimuli.[54] In the reshaping of the maternal brain, old is replaced with new, as the brain never returns to the connective pathways it held before motherhood.

Postnatal neurogenesis is found to target all regions of the brain, but the most important changes for attachment take place in the hippocampus, the amygdala, and the hypothalamus. An increase in functional connectivity in the hippocampal and amygdalaic regions facilitates faster behavioural and emotional response rates. The significance of quick responses is evolutionary in that it allows for the mother to meet her baby's physical needs in a timely manner. Furthermore, the involvement of hippocampal neurons boosts her memory encoding and retrieval abilities. The more she engages in the relational dance with the child, the more adept she becomes at recognizing her baby's specific needs and unique ways of communicating. It is as if the prenatally acquired vigilance is finally put into action to assure bonding in postnatal separation. The mother's efficient learning abilities and responsiveness ultimately contribute to a long-lasting bond with the child and assure mutual wellbeing.

As some parts of the brain are becoming more sensitive, other regions are found to tone down their activity. Interestingly, the hypothalamic-pituitary axis (HPA) becomes less responsive to stressors in the postpartum period.[55] Schmidt et al. (2003) discovered that during the first two postnatal weeks, female mice became resistant to cortisol release in novel situations and in response to stressful stimuli. Their lowered stress response was characterized by an increase in central regulator hormone activity in the hypothalamus. Lower levels of cortisol help cope with postnatal stress by giving the mother access to a calm and even fearless mental disposition. The mother's hypo-responsive period is useful in regulating her own as well as her child's arousal states. As stated by Gerhardt (2004), the mitigation of cortisol release in the young foetal nervous system is a prerequisite for secure attachment bonds and cannot be established without co-regulation with the primary caregiver.[56] Co-regulation in the early weeks means responding to the baby's coos and cries, breastfeeding, holding the baby close, and even making eye-contact. The more mental resources the mother can dedicate to such care-taking behaviours, the more the foetal nervous system is enriched by trust and safety. In sum, the mother's neurochemical system supports taking care of the child after birth.

Conclusion

The emergence of love as a neurochemical process of mother/child attachment begins with pregnancy and continues to years after birth. During this time, a process of co-regulation in the dyad leads to a condition of homeostasis. The dance of the dyad is delicate, because the mother is not conscious of her impact on the foetal nervous system, and the foetus has yet to gain control over sensory stimuli. An expecting mother's navigation of environmental stressors shapes her child's nervous system. The young nervous system begins to mirror maternal arousal states, as it develops the ability to regulate independently. This co-regulation process lays a foundation for attachment by giving the foetus access to its first experiences of safety.

The mother has an in-built biological toolkit that supports creating a safe environment for the child. In pregnancy, her cognitive capacities for caretaking intensify as grey axonal matter in the brain decreases. Due to this shift in resource allocation, her ability to dedicate cognitive effort to caretaking increases, preparing her to protect herself and the child during pregnancy and after. The mother's awakening vigilance is complemented by a surge in pregnancy hormone production. Specifically, progesterone and estrogen act as agents of attachment by enhancing the pleasure response; social affiliation and affectionate behaviours begin to feel more rewarding, encouraging continued attunement to the foetal presence. From the moment of conception to the moment of birth, the unconscious and molecular units of life are oriented to nurture the attachment bond that forms between mother and child.

Through a neurochemical lens, it may be said that *love* is a deeply rooted biological phenomenon with profound implications for human development.

Endnotes

1. The original version of this paper written to fit commonly acceptable academic standards has been published separately by the Guerrand-Hermès Foundation for Peace. This version has been edited to fit the style of the Position Paper.
2. Kinsey, C., & Hupcey, J. (2013). State of the science of maternal-infant bonding: a principle-based concept analysis. *Midwifery*, 29(12). doi: 10.1016/j.midw.2012.12.019.
3. American Psychological Association. (2017). Ethical principles of psychologists and code of conduct (2002, amended effective June 1, 2010, and January 1, 2017). http://www.apa.org/ethics/code/
4. Gerhardt, S. (2004). *Why Love Matters: How Affection Shapes a Baby's Brain*. Routledge Publishing, Oxford.
5. Hardy, S. (2004). Evolutionary context of human development: the cooperative breeding model. *Attachment and Bonding: A New Synthesis*. Cambridge: M.I.T. Press.
6. Harlow, H. F. & Zimmermann, R. R. (1958). The development of affective responsiveness in infant monkeys. *Proceedings of the American Philosophical Society*, 102, 501 -509.
7. Fromm, E. (1956). *The Art of Loving*. Thorsons, Dublin.
8. Hanazawa, H. (2022). Polyvagal theory and its clinical potential: an overview. *Brain and Nerve*, 78(8), 1011-1016. doi: 10.11477/mf.1416202169.
9. Porges, S. (2017). *The Pocket Guide to the Polyvagal Theory: The Transformative Power of Feeling Safe*. W. W. Norton & Company.
10. Porges, S. & Furman, S. (2011). The Early Development of the Autonomic Nervous Provides a Neural Platform for Social Behavior: A Polyvagal Perspective. *Infant Child Development*, 20(1), 106-118. doi: 10.1002/icd.688.
11. Searle, J. R. (2000). Consciousness. *Annual Review of Neuroscience*, 23(1), 557–578. doi: 10.1146/annurev.

	neuro.23.1.557.
12	Swimme, B. (2019). *Hidden Heart of the Cosmos*. Orbis Publishing.
13	"Foetal Awareness: Review of Research and Recommendations for Practice". (2010). Royal College of Obstetricians and Gynaecologists.
14	Giannakoulopoulos, X., et al. (1999). Human foetal and maternal noradrenaline responses to invasive procedures. *Pediatric Research*, 45(1), 494–499.
15	Baars, B., et al. (2021). Global Workspace Theory (GWT) and Prefrontal Cortex: Recent Developments. *Frontiers in Psychology*, 10. doi: 10.3389/fpsyg.2021.749868.
16	"Executive Function". (2023). Harvard University Center on the Developing Child. Retrieved from developingchild.harvard.edu/science/key-concepts/executive-function/
17	Smith, L., & Kisilevsky, B. (2007). Estimated cardiac vagal tone predicts foetal responses to mother's and stranger's voices. *Developmental Psychobiology*, 49(5), 543-547. doi:10.1002/dev.20229.
18	Wilson, S., et al. (2021). Development of human white matter pathways in utero over the second and third trimester. *PNAS*, 118(20). doi: 10.1073/pnas.202359811.
19	Feng, K., et al. (2019). Diffusion Tensor MRI of White Matter of Healthy Full-term Newborns: Relationship to Neurodevelopmental Outcomes. *Radiology*, 292(1). doi: 10.1148/radiol.2019182564.
20	Kasser, S., et al. (2019). Birth experience in newborn infants is associated with changes in nociceptive sensitivity. *Scientific Reports*, 9(4117). doi: 10.1038/s41598-019-40650-2.
21	Lagercrantz, H., & Changeux, J.P. (2010). Basic consciousness of the newborn. *Seminars in Perinatology*, 34(3), 201–206. doi: 10.1053/j.semperi.2010.02.004.
22	Sakai, J. (2020). How synaptic pruning shapes neural wiring during development and, possibly, in disease. PNAS, 117(28). doi: 10.1073/pnas.2010281117.
23	McMurray, B. (2014). Neonatal speech perception. *Journal of Cognition*, 129(2), 362-78. doi: 10.1016/j.

cognition.2013.07.015.

24 Feng et al. (2019). Diffusion Tensor MRI of White Matter of Healthy Full-term Newborns: Relationship to Neurodevelopmental Outcomes. *Radiology*, 292(1). doi: 10.1148/radiol.2019182564; Balasundaram, P., & Avulakunta, I.D. (2022). *Bayley Scales Of Infant and Toddler Development*. StatPearls Publishing, FL. Retrieved from www.ncbi.nlm.nih.gov/books/NBK567715/

25 Kirsch, M., & Buchholz, M. (2020). On the Nature of the Mother-Infant Tie and Its Interaction With Freudian Drives. *Frontiers in Psychology*, 11(317). doi: 10.3389/fpsyg.2020.00317.

26 Suttie, I. (1988). *The origins of love and hate*. Free Association Books.

27 Feldman, R., & Eidelman, A. (2007). Maternal postpartum behaviour and the emergence of infant-mother and infant-father synchrony in preterm and full-term infants: the role of neonatal vagal tone. *Developmental Psychobiology*. 49, 290–302. doi: 10.1002/dev.20220.

28 Hoekzema, E., et al. (2016). Pregnancy leads to long-lasting changes in human brain structure. *Nature Neuroscience*, 20(2), 287-296. doi: 10.1038/nn.4458.

29 Hoekzema, E., et al. (2022). Mapping the effects of pregnancy on resting state brain activity, white matter microstructure, neural metabolite concentrations and grey matter architecture. *Nature Communications*, 13(6931). doi: 10.1038/s41467-022-33884-8.

30 Trombetta, T., et al. (2021). Pre-natal Attachment and Parent-To-Infant Attachment: A Systematic Review. *Frontiers in Psychology*, 12(3). doi: 10.3389/fpsyg.2021.620942.

31 "Brain Reward Pathways". (2018). Icahn School of Medicine at Mount Sinai. neuroscience.mssm.edu/nestler/nidappg/brain_reward_pathways.html.

32 McCarthy, M. (1995). Estrogen modulation of oxytocin and its relation to behaviour. *Advances in experimental medicine and biology*, 395, 235-45.

33 Nissensson, R., Flouret, G., & Hechter, O. (1978).

Opposing effects of estradiol and progesterone on oxytocin receptors in rabbit uterus. *PNAS*, 75(4). doi: 10.1073/pnas.75.4.2044.

34 Aschbacher, K., et al. (2013). Good Stress, Bad Stress and Oxidative Stress: Insights from Anticipatory Cortisol Reactivity. *Psychoneuroendocrinology*, 38(9), 1698–1708. doi: 10.1016/j.psyneuen.2013.02.004.

35 Samet, J. & Wages, P. (2018). Oxidative Stress from Environmental Exposures. *Current Opinion in Toxicology*, 6, 60-66.

36 Fan, F., et al. (2018). The relationship between maternal anxiety and cortisol during pregnancy and birth weight of Chinese neonates. *BMC Pregnancy and Childbirth*, 18(265). doi: 10.1186/s12884-018-1798-x; Keller-Wood, M., et al. (2014). Elevated maternal cortisol leads to relative maternal hyperglycaemia and increased stillbirth in ovine pregnancy. *American Journal of Physiology*, 307(4). doi: 10.1152/ajpregu.00530.2013.

37 Van Leeuwen, P., et al. (2009). Influence of paced maternal breathing on foetal–maternal heart rate coordination. *PNAS*, 106(33). doi: 10.1073/pnas.090104910.

38 O'Donoghue, K. (2008). Foetal microchimerism and maternal health during and after pregnancy. *Obstetric Medicine*, 1(2), 56-64, doi: 10.1258/om.2008.080008.

39 Boddy, A., et al. (2015). Foetal microchimerism and maternal health: A review and evolutionary analysis of cooperation and conflict beyond the womb. *Bioessays*, 37(10), 1106-1118. doi: 10.1002/bies.201500059.

40 Haig, D. (2019). Cooperation and conflict in human pregnancy. *Current Biology*, 29(11), 455-458. doi: 10.1016/j.cub.2019.04.040.

41 Geno, A., et al. (2021). *Handbook of Diagnostic Endocrinology*, 543-579. doi: 10.1016/B978-0-12-818277-2.00015-7.

42 Fox, H. & Sebire, N. (2007). *Pathology of the Placenta*, 57-67. Elsevier Science Publishers.

43 Kinsley, C., et al. (2014). The mother as hunter: Significant reduction in foraging costs through enhancements of

	predation in maternal rats. *Hormones and Behavior,* 66(4), 649-654.
44	Byrne, S., et al. (2019). Facial emotion recognition during pregnancy: Examining the effects of facial age and affect. *Infant Behavioural Development,* 54, pp.108-113. doi: 10.1016/j.infbeh.2018.09.008.
45	Takubo et al. (2022). Relationship between Antenatal Mental Health and Facial Emotion Recognition Bias for Children's Faces among Pregnant Women. *Journal of Personalized Medicine,* 12(9). doi: 10.3390/jpm12091391.
46	Pearson, R., Lightman, S., & Evans, J. (2009). Emotional sensitivity for motherhood: Late pregnancy is associated with enhanced accuracy to encode emotional faces. *Hormones and Behavior,* 56(5), 557–563. doi: 10.1016/j.yhbeh.2009.09.013.
47	National Child & Maternal Health Education Program. (2023). *Know Your Terms: Full-Term Pregnancy.* www.nichd.nih.gov/ncmhep/initiatives/know-your-terms/moms.
48	Gao, L., et al. (2015). Steroid receptor coactivators 1 and 2 mediate foetal-to-maternal signalling that initiates parturition. *Journal of Clinical Investigation.* doi: 10.1172/JCI78544.
49	Osilla, E. & Sharma, S. (2021). *Oxytocin.* StatPearls Publishing, FL.
50	Sprouse-Blum, A. (2010). Understanding Endorphins and Their Importance in Pain Management. *Hawai'i Medical Journal,* 69(3), 70-71.
51	Dahan, O. (2020). Birthing Consciousness as a Case of Adaptive Altered State of Consciousness Associated with Transient Hypofrontality. *Association for Psychological Science,* 15(3). doi: 10.1177/1745691620901546.
52	Ong, W., Stohler, C., and Herr, D. (2019). Role of the Prefrontal Cortex in Pain Processing. *Molecular Neurobiology,* 56(2), 1137–1166. doi: 10.1007/s12035-018-1130-9.
53	Costa-Martins, J. M., et al. (2014). Attachment styles, pain, and the consumption of analgesics during labour: a prospective observational study. *The Journal of Pain,* 15(3),

304-311. doi: 10.1016/j.jpain.2013.12.004.
54 Leuner, B. & Sabihi, S. (2016). The birth of new neurons in the maternal brain: hormonal regulation and functional implications. *Frontiers in Neuroendocrinology*, 41, 99-113. doi: 10.1016/j.yfrne.2016.02.004.
55 Schmidt, M., et al. (2006). The postnatal development of the hypothalamic-pituitary-adrenal axis in the mouse. International *Journal of Developmental Neuroscience*, 24(4). doi: 10.1016/s0736-5748(03)00030-3.
56 Gerhardt, S. (2004). *Why Love Matters: How Affection Shapes a Baby's Brain*. Routledge Publishing, Oxford.

Appendix 3:

Love and the Tao

As I have suggested before, one of the difficulties of engaging with the enquiry of *In Order to Love* [2] has been the matter of language. However much we may try to challenge conventions, we are to some extent trapped in the dominant language and perceptions of our time. In this respect, and seeking a different way of seeing and speaking, I have been greatly assisted by the Tao whose teachings provide 'another language', a unique presentation of a world in which relationships and connections are paramount. I set out below some brief thoughts on why this is so.

Some years ago, I was introduced to the Taoist Master Christopher Chuang, who encouraged me to return to a translation of *The Tao* that was sitting on one of my bookshelves. It was a translation by Stephen Mitchell.[3] Since then I have read a number of other translations,[4] each of which has its own merits, but I still go back to Mitchell's translation as my primary source, with the translation by Ursula Le Guin as an alternative.

And what do I find?

We begin *The Tao* with an important an somewhat daunting verse, which tells us that there is nothing that can be said about the Tao, since the Tao is beyond words. So, although we wish to know the Tao, we find ourselves without any words that are adequate. The same can be said of Love. Here, too, we often find that we are lost for words. And yet, in our work together Master Chuang and I began to see that although, in most translations, Love is seldom spoken of, it is possible to see that Love is the energy of the Tao, or rather perhaps it is the movement of the Tao, from and towards. Or perhaps.... But then, you see, we are once more caught in the inadequacy of words. Nevertheless, both Master Chuang and I found ourselves wanting to say something about this, or perhaps to be able to point towards what might be said.

As we see in Chapter 1 of this Position Statement, we are told by cosmologists, or at least by some of them, that everything that is is interconnected and part of a whole, our world, our Universe, the cosmos. Another way of seeing this is to say that the whole is the Tao, and the fabric of the interconnection is Love, the weave, the flow of waters from a Divine spring, running through streams and rivers back to the ocean of Oneness.

In *The Tao*, it is said that from Oneness comes Twoness, the *yin* and *yang* in apparent opposition before the coming of Threeness, a reconciliation through Love and the arising of all that is:

> The Tao gives birth to One.
> One gives birth to Two.
> Two gives birth to Three.
> Three gives birth to all things.[5]

For, says the Tao:

> Man follows the earth.
> Earth follows the universe.
> The universe follows the Tao.
> The Tao follows only itself.[6]

And, speaking with voice of Love, we might say:

> And the following is Love,
> And that which follows is Love.

Or in those words of Love that were spoken to me almost ten years ago:

> Being and Love are a constant rhythm of union, separation and reunion – the essential qualities of Being, held in balance and harmony by Love.[7]

It is the Tao that tells us that we need to be in touch with Love. Only in Love can the path of the Tao be discerned, be known and, as a wave, become manifest in the energy of life – expressed in Nature. Look all around you. Listen to the Silence in the night, for it is from loving Darkness that Light arises. Indeed, as soon as Love is named it has gone, gone back into the darkness from whence it came. So, in the voice of Love, we might say:

> Follow with love,
> but do not follow.
> Love is always waiting for you,
> there in the darkness.
>
> Make some tea.
> Offer it to a friend,
> and set it down.
> Ask her:
> "Would you like cake?"
>
> Everything is Love.
> And Love is nowhere to be seen.
>
> The tide is rising and falling.
> The moon grows large and small.
> The sun arises from the East,
> and sets in the West.
> The breeze runs through the reed bed.

Love at work

Thinking of the needs of Love, I turn, once again, to Mitchell's translation of the first stanza of Chapter 1 of *The Tao Te Ching*, where he says:

> The tao that can be told
> is not the eternal Tao.
> The name that can be named
> is not the eternal Name.[8]

At once I am caught off guard, for my own Western culture insists on naming and knowing, on possessing and controlling. What must I do?

The answer is that I must listen and explore what Ursula Le Guin calls a "Mystery of all mysteries!/The door to the hidden."[9] Stephen

Mitchell translates this as follows:

> Yet mystery and manifestations
> arise from the same source.
> This source is called darkness.
>
> Darkness within darkness.
> The gateway to all understanding.[10]

There is something here about our need to form a relationship with darkness if we are to understand the mysteries of the Tao and therefore, by the same cause, the mysteries of Love. By contrast to the Christian, and indeed the Quaker, emphasis on The Light, darkness as the "gateway to all understanding" is exactly what I have found in my own pondering, and to find it expressed in this way in *The Tao* is very reassuring. Rosemarie Anderson translates it as follows:

> Dark beyond dark is
> The door to all subtleties.[11]

The Tao is thought to have been written down in China by Lao-Tzu some time in the last five hundred years BC. Nothing much is known about Lao-Tzu, but he was probably the archive-keeper of one of the small kingdoms of his time,[12] and he may have been an older contemporary of Confucius. Some regard the verses as a treatise on the art of government, whilst others find it to be more of a philosophy of life.[13] In any event, it offers a way of perceiving ourselves and our relationships with each other, our loving relationships with each other, that is quite contrary to present Western culture. It is not, as is sometimes supposed, simply a treatise on not-doing, not at all, rather it is a teaching of doing in ways that are integrated and self-less, where "we can't tell the dancer from the dance."[14] There is a softness and a gentleness to the teachings, but also a strength and a firmness and, says Mitchell,[15] of all the great teachings, those of Lao-Tzu are "by far the most female." Mitchell uses both the feminine and the masculine in his description of the Tao:

The Tao is called the Great Mother:
empty yet inexhaustible,
it gives birth to infinite worlds.[16]

Indeed, Rosemarie Anderson, who, in her early thirties, travelled to Asia and studied the etymology of Chinese characters, says this:

To my surprise, I discovered that the Tao was profoundly feminine! Never could I have predicted that because, in the English translations I read, the Tao is commonly referred to as 'It' throughout the poems. How could so many translators, almost all men, not have noticed that the Tao is consistently referred to as 'mother', 'virgin', and 'womb of creation', all of which are clearly feminine and hardly gender neutral?... I could not possibly refer to the Tao as anything other than 'She'.[17]

And later, in a section titled 'The Divine Feminine Tao', she says:

The tenderness and hiddenness of the Tao signal Her Feminine nature...Not only is the Tao's nature uniquely feminine, but creation is described as a solo act rooted in the immortal void, the dark womb. Endlessly returning to source, all creation passes through her womb and then into the world.[18]

Yielding not dominating is the way of both Love and the Tao,[19] which nourishes and completes all things.[20] As Ursula Le Guin has it:

The Way is hidden
in its namelessness.
But only the Way
begins, sustains, fulfils.

In the voice of Love, this might be:

The way of Love is hidden
in its namelessness.

But only the Way of Love
begins, sustains, fulfils.[21]

And then it seems clear that for the Tao, and therefore for Love, there is always integration: for it is said in *The Tao* that when male and female combine, all things achieve harmony.[22] I note that these words are akin to the later gnostic teachings in the Gospel of Thomas, that "when you make the female into a single One so that the male is not the male and the female is not the female…then you will enter the Kingdom."[23]

The Tao, says Lao-Tzu is the mother of all things:

The Tao gives birth to all beings,
nourishes them, maintains them,
cares for them, comforts them, protects them,
takes them back to itself,
creating without possessing,
acting without expecting,
guiding without interfering.
That is why love of the Tao
is the very nature of things.[24]

And if this is so, then to understand what Love requires of us, we must also see and follow Love's characteristics of nourishing and caring, of comforting and protecting. If Lao-Tzu is here speaking of the Tao, he might also be talking of Love:

The Tao is always at ease.
It overcomes without competing,
answers without speaking a word,
arrives without being summoned,
accomplishes without a plan.[25]

The Tao is full of compassion:

I have just three things to teach:
simplicity, patience, compassion.[26]

And so it would seem that this, too, is what Love requires of us, being at ease, and full of compassion. Indeed, the Tao offers us 'another language', a language of integration, connection and relationship. And as I read it, in its many versions, I begin to see that the Tao is Love. And if there is nothing that can be said about the Tao since the Tao is beyond words, perhaps the same can be said of Love. In such a place, we come to Silence, resting there and watching Love flow through us. For like the Tao, Love is the energy that brings together and sets apart, or rather it is the movement of the Tao, from and to. Or.... But then, you see, we are caught once more in words.

And so we come to Silence as a source of Love.

This April morning, the sycamore tree is coming into leaf, seeming not to move, still and silent. Then I notice it. There is movement, very slight at the very edge, caught in a light breeze coming from the south. The silence remains and radiates from the tree far out into the universe and then into the cosmos and beyond into the Tao. It is as if, in its constant flowing of birth and rebirth, the sycamore is saying:

> Look at me, see how my flourishing returns, again and again.
> You have watched me resting through the winter, sparse,
> waiting. And now, once more, I begin to blossom. Can you feel
> my energy returning?

All is well.

In September 2022, I took part in a webinar being organized in China by Master Chuang. In that webinar, I spoke, once more, of Love as being of the essence, and afterwards a number of those who had been at the webinar asked how they might take what I had said into to the daily practise of their lives. Having spoken to Master Chuang about this, we decided that we and his community of students, should gather together once a week in a Time of Silence, for we felt sure that in that action of simple Silence we would find a place for Love to become manifest.

On 5th March 2023, the first Time of Silence took place on Zoom and was well attended. It was deliberately simple. Master Chuang began by welcoming the eighty or so participants to the twenty minutes of Silence and, at the end, I thanked everyone for coming, saying that we intended to repeat our practice for a further three weeks, meeting on the Sunday at the same time of each week. After each gathering those attending were invited to share comments and questions, Master Chuang's colleague, Yimi Mao, collecting them together and sending them to him and to me for comment and to provide, as best we could, answers to the questions.

To begin with there was some unfamiliarity with sitting in silence, but, quite quickly, the participants began to feel comfortable and, indeed, spoke of how the Silence was nourishing them. The main questions were about either the practice itself or about how this matter of Love could be found in everyday lives.

The Time of Silence practice, which Master Chuang and I have offered to his community of students, is a gentle form of reflection upon Love, and it is based upon the premise that Love is of the essence, and that Silence and Stillness open a space for Love to come to us so that we are governed by Love in all we say and do, in *all* we say and do. We do this not only for ourselves, but for our family, our community and, indeed, for the Earth and the Universe. Each one of these benefit from the practice. We do this because we have come to understand that the Way of Love is the underlying intention of our Universe, which is always seeking to move to higher and higher levels of consciousness, higher and higher levels of Love over very long periods of time – Love, through Love to Great Love. Great Love is calling us towards Great Love. And we must ask, are we nourishing this in the deepest parts of us, and are we making ourselves ready for this? Or do we think it is absurd and turn our backs on it? And does it matter if we do? It does.

The practice of the Time of Silence is very simple and should be undertaken gently. Those coming to it are urged to find a quiet place and sit comfortably, sitting in an upright position with their hands resting, or cupped, upon their thighs. They can close their eyes or keep them open, whichever they prefer. Coming into the Silence we are invited to be still and be without any expectation as to what we will find or receive, giving ourselves to the Silence, open to the coming of Love.

To begin with, we may find that our mind is agitated, one thought and then another arising. If so, we are asked to just look at these thoughts and let them go, trying not to follow their story, but to watch the coming and going of our breath, breathing in and then breathing out and lingering on the outbreath. We learn to breathe deeply, taking the inbreath into our belly and then to our chest, letting the outbreath pass easily though our lips. We are taught not to hurry, and if thoughts arise, to let them go and come back to our breath. At the end of twenty minutes, a bowl is struck and the Time of Silence come to an end.

Those who intentionally continue with this practise find that, as they move their focus from their head to their heart, their hearts begin to open to make a space for Love to come to them. They rest there and wait *without expectation*, being kind and gentle with themselves, so that, in time, they learn, by habit, to become kind and gentle in all they say and do.

Place the palm of your right hand over your heart, close your eyes and feel the energy coming to you, finding its way to you. Return to the breath.

For in *The Tao* it is said:

Therefore the Master
acts without doing anything
and teaches without saying anything.
Things arise and she lets them come;
Things disappear and she lets them go.
She has but doesn't possess,
acts but doesn't expect.
When her work is done, she forgets it.
That is why it lasts forever.[27]

Which in the language of Love, is to say this:

Therefore Love
acts without doing anything
and teaches without saying anything.
Things arise and Love lets them come;
things disappear and Love lets them go.

> Love does not possess,
> acts but doesn't expect.
> When Love's work is done, Love forgets it.
> That is why it lasts forever.

This is the practice of the Time of Silence, to be quiet and still so that Love can arise and 'teach without saying anything'.

So, once more, in terms of exploring that which Love requires in order to be manifest, this work on the Tao with Master Chuang, and the practise of Time of Silence, suggests that Love will come to us when we are ready to receive, when for even a moment, a breath or a pause, we become silent and still, when we stop searching and simply open our hearts to the possibility of Love, waiting without expectation so that we no longer grasp at what it is we think we need, but become ready for it to come to us.

In case it is thought that such a readiness is too passive, I would only say that I have found that the way of being that Love requires, needs deliberate intention and discipline, lest we unknowingly prevent Love. Our silent practice needs to be deepened by regular practise until our intention becomes our habit.

Silence may nourish us, but not always. There is the silence of anger and disapproval, the silence of hatred and distaste. But these are all made by us when we move away from Love. We may abandon Love, but Love never abandons us. Indeed, the true Silence of Love, timeless and universal, precedes us, and is there for us, ever close by. We must simply turn towards it. It is for us to find our way to Love, surrendering ourselves to it, just like the sycamore tree. As is said by *The Tao*:

> The supreme good is like water,
> which nourishes all things without trying to.
> It is content with the low places that people disdain.
> Thus it is like the Tao.[28]

Endnotes

1. Parts of this text come from David Cadman, *The Recovery of Love*, Zig Publishing, 2022, Chapter 9.
2. See Chapter 1 of The Recovery of Love.
3. Lao-Tzu, *Tao Te Ching: The Book of the Way*, Translated by Stephen Mitchell, Kyle Cathie, 1988.
4. Lao-Tzu, *Tao Te Ching: A Book About The Way and the Power of the Way*, translated by Ursula K. Le Guin, Shambala, 1998; *The Tao Te Ching: A New Translation with Commentary*, translated by Ellen M. Chen, Paragon House, 1989; *The Divine Feminine Tao Te Ching: A New Translation & Commentary*, translated by Rosemarie Anderson, Inner Traditions, 2021.
5. Lao-Tzu, *Tao Te Ching: The Book of the Way*, Translated by Stephen Mitchell, Kyle Cathie, 1988, Chapter 42.
6. Ibid. Chapter. 25.
7. David Cadman, *Love and the Divine Feminine*, Panacea Books, 2020, 7.
8. Lao-Tzu, *Tao Te Ching: The Book of the Way*, Translated by Stephen Mitchell, Kyle Cathie, 1988, Chapter 1.
9. Lao-Tzu, *Tao Te Ching: A Book About The Way and the Power of the Way*, translated by Ursula K. Le Guin, Shambala, 1998, Chapter 1.
10. Lao-Tzu, *Tao Te Ching: The Book of the Way*, Translated by Stephen Mitchell, Kyle Cathie, 1988, Chapter 1.
11. *The Divine Feminine Tao Te Ching: A New Translation & Commentary*, translated by Rosemarie Anderson, Inner Traditions, 2021, Chapter 1.
12. Lao-Tzu, *Tao Te Ching: The Book of the Way*, Translated by Stephen Mitchell, Kyle Cathie, 1988, Stephen Mitchell, vii.
13. Ibid.
14. Ibid.
15. Ibid. ix.
16. Ibid. Chapter 6.
17. *The Divine Feminine Tao Te Ching: A New Translation &*

	Commentary, translated by Rosemarie Anderson, Inner Traditions, 2021, 3.
18	Ibid. 11.
19	Ibid. Chapter 40.
20	Ibid. Chapter 41.
21	Lao-Tzu, *Tao Te Ching: A Book About The Way and the Power of the Way*, translated by Ursula K. Le Guin, Shambala, 1998, Chapter 41.
22	Lao-Tzu, *Tao Te Ching: The Book of the Way*, Translated by Stephen Mitchell, Kyle Cathie, 1988, Stephen Mitchell, Chapter 42.
23	*The Gospel of Thomas*, translated by Jean-Yves Leloup and translated into English by Joseph Rowe, Inner Traditions, 1986, 19.
24	Lao-Tzu, *Tao Te Ching: The Book of the Way*, Translated by Stephen Mitchell, Kyle Cathie, 1988, Stephen Mitchell, Kyle Cathie, 1988. Chapter 51.
25	Ibid. Chapter 73.
26	Ibid. Chapter 67.
27	Ibid. Chapter 2.
28	Ibid. Chapter 8.

Appendix 4:

Bibliography

(IN TOPIC AND DATE ORDER)

1. LOVE

Why Love Matters: Values in Governance, complied and edited by Scherto Gill and David Cadman, Peter Lang, 2016.

David Cadman, *Love and the Divine Feminine*, Panacea Books, 2020.

David Cadman, *The Recovery of Love: Living in a Troubled World*, Zig Publishing, 2022.

Scherto Gill, *Lest We Lose Love: Rediscovering the Core of Western Culture*, Anthem Press, 2023.

2. COSMOLOGY

Pierre Teilhard de Chardin, *Le Phénomènon Humaine*, translated by Sarah Appleton-Weber, Oxford University Press, 1999.

Brian Swimme, *The Universe Is a Green Dragon: A Cosmic Creation Story*, Bear & Company, 2001

Jude Currivan, *The 8th Chakra: What It Is and How It Can Transform Your Life*, Hay House, 2006 and 2012.

Louis M. Savary and Patricia H. Berne, *Teilhard de Chardin on Love*, Paulist Press, New York, 2017.

Louis M. Savary, *Teilhard de Chardin's The Phenomenon of Man Explained*, Paulist Press, 2020.

Brian Swimme, *Cosmogenesis: An Unveiling of the Expanding Universe*, Counterpoint, 2022.

Jude Currivan, *The Cosmic Hologram: In-formation at the Center of Creation*, Inner Traditions, 2017.

John F. Haught, *the New Cosmic Story: Inside Our Awakening Universe*, Yale University Press, 2017.

John F. Haught, *The Cosmic Vision of Teilhard de Chardin*, Orbis Books, 2021.

Jude Currivan PhD, *The Story of Gaia: The Big Breath and the Evolutionary Journey of Our Conscious Planet*, Inner Traditions, 2022.

3. CONSCIOUSNESS

Rupert Spira, *The Transparency of Things: Contemplating the Nature of Experience*, Sahaja Publications, 2016.

Rupert Spira, *The Nature of Consciousness: Essays on the Unity of Mind and Matter*, Sahaja, 2017.

Rupert Spira, *The Heart of Prayer*, Sahaja Publications, 2023.

4. THE TAO

Lao-Tzu, *Tao Te Ching: The Book of the Way*, Translated by Stephen Mitchell, Kyle Cathie, 1988.

Lao-Tzu, *Tao Te Ching: A Book About The Way and the Power of the Way*, translated by Ursula K. Le Guin, Shambala, 1998.

The Tao Te Ching: A New Translation with Commentary, translated by Ellen M. Chen, Paragon House, 1989.

The Divine Feminine Tao Te Ching: A New Translation & Commentary, translated by Rosemarie Anderson, Inner Traditions, 2021.

5. OTHER

The Gospel of Thomas, translated by Jean-Yves Leloup and translated into English by Joseph Rowe, Inner Traditions, 1986.

Humberto Maturana Romesin and Gerda Verden-Zoller, *The Origin of Humanness*, Edited by Pille Bunnell, Imprint Academic, 2008.

Kenneth Gergen, *Relational Being: Beyond Self and Community*, Oxford University Press, 2009.

Iain McGilchrist, *The Master and His Emissary: The Divided Brain and the Making of the Western World*, Yale University Press, first published in 2010 and republished in 2018.

Rutger Bregman, *Human Kind: A Hopeful History*, Bloomsbury, 2012, first published in 2020.

Printed in Great Britain
by Amazon